MW00617896

It's All
In Your Head,
Kathleen!

A Memoir of a Medical Victory!

KATHLEEN FRIES

LifeRich Publishing is a registered trademark of The Reader's Digest Association, Inc.

LifeRich Publishing books may be ordered through booksellers or by contacting:

LifeRich Publishing
1663 Liberty Drive
Bloomington, IN 47403
www.liferichpublishing.com
844-686-9607

ISBN: 978-1-4897-4903-1 (sc)
ISBN: 978-1-4897-4904-8 (hc)
ISBN: 978-1-4897-4908-6 (e)

Library of Congress Control Number: 2023916844

Print information available on the last page.

LifeRich Publishing rev. date: 10/02/2023

ACKNOWLEDGMENTS

To Julie, my friend and neighbor, who aided me in editing my original manuscript. She was instrumental in helping me prepare this book's first draft for submission.

To Richard, my friend and technical support, who without his assistance I would have been lost.

To Ken, my cheerleader, who constantly encouraged me to pursue what I started and see it through.

To my family and friends, who helped me laugh and try to stay positive when it became difficult to do so.

You are all my angels in this call and endeavor. This was a labor of love, and my story, which I felt compelled to share.

Thank You,
Kathy

CONTENTS

PREFACE

Did you ever have something happen to you in your life when you felt a nudge or urge to share what was happening to you with others? I have felt nudged to share my story several times over the last few years while on this journey of unexplained physical and mental changes that eventually led me to a diagnosis and treatment for a condition called Normal Pressure Hydrocephalus (NPH). Normal Pressure Hydrocephalus is a condition in which excess cerebrospinal fluid builds up in the chambers, or ventricles of the brain. When too much fluid fills these ventricles, they press against the brain tissue which can lead to damage. This damage shows up in a variety of physical and cognitive symptoms. Treatment can involve placing a shunt to drain the excess fluid away from the brain.

In an attempt to raise awareness and perhaps help others, I decided to share my story of how I went from looking at possibly entering a nursing home with a diagnosis of dementia to regaining the life I had enjoyed previously. My experience made me wonder how many people might be resigned to living out the rest of their lives languishing in nursing homes who could, with the correct diagnosis, benefit from the placement of a ventricular peritoneal (VP) shunt as I have done.

This book is a memoir of the events that took me by surprise after many years of wondering what was happening to me. Were these symptoms the beginning of dementia or the dreaded "A" word–Alzheimer's disease–or something else that could explain so many declining symptoms? And if it was something else, could it be treated?

I consider myself lucky to live in Cincinnati, Ohio where we have the University of Cincinnati (UC) Gardner Neuroscience Institute. Through a series of unfortunate events, which ultimately turned out to be fortunate for me, I was led to Dr. Alberto Espay, a motion disorder specialist at UC Gardner who works with patients who have Parkinson's disease and with patients suffering from the effects of NPH. Thanks to him and a senior resident in neurosurgery at UC Medical Center, I was able to, after more than three years of specialists and testing, eventually get my diagnosis and treatment. On December 11, 2020, in the middle of the Covid-19 pandemic, I had a VP shunt placed and my life was changed.

This is the story of how long it took me to reach the place where medical professionals decided to go ahead and perform the procedure that ended up changing my life. I went in with many symptoms that had greatly altered my life and was told that a shunt would probably not fix them all. But what was most important to me was the possibility of improving my balance, walking, changes in mental status, and incontinence issues.

My purpose in writing about my experience is to be informative and helpful to others in a similar situation. Hopefully, this information will help you to research NPH and discover if a VP shunt might be beneficial for you or a family member who may be struggling to get answers about this sometimes difficult to diagnose condition called Normal Pressure Hydrocephalus.

Before getting into the details of the symptoms I was experiencing and the process of getting diagnosed and treated, I would like to start at the beginning and share some family history.

1

Family History

I was born in 1951, the youngest of four girls, to Ed and Sylvia Doherty. We were a normal Irish Catholic family growing up in the Price Hill neighborhood of Cincinnati, Ohio. My father was a pressman for a local printing company. We weren't poor, he made enough for us to get by, but we weren't wealthy by any means. My mother was the type who made sure we were nicely dressed and stretched money so that we never knew any hardships. Our parents made us all feel special, comfortable, and loved. We all went to Catholic grade schools and Seton High School, an all-girls Catholic school in our Price Hill neighborhood. Granted, the tuition was nothing like it is today, but it put added expense and stress on the family to afford the extra costs. My mother didn't drive so she took on part-time telephone sales jobs so that she could earn some money to pay for extras while working from home.

In 1954, my parents purchased a small white house in Price Hill after renting for years due to a fear of not being able to afford their own home. It was not long after we moved in that my sister Sylvia contracted polio at the age of 12, ultimately impacting the entire family.

Before polio vaccines became available, several polio epidemics occurred between 1948 and 1955. According to the Centers for Disease Control and Prevention (CDC), between 1950 and 1953 there were approximately 119,000 cases of paralytic polio and 6,600 deaths in the United States. Some people, especially infants and young children, were asymptomatic or had mild symptoms. However for some, it resulted in paralysis or at times, death. Depending on how the brain and spinal cord were affected, the paralysis could affect movement and strength of the arms, legs, and the muscles required for breathing.

The virus was highly contagious and transmission peaked during the summer months, causing cities to close swimming pools and people to stay home. It was a frightening time during these summers as parents waited fearfully to see if it would strike. One day you may have a headache and hours later you could wind up paralyzed.

Unfortunately for my family, it struck my sister Sylvia. My mother was devastated. She had some theories about how Sylvia had picked up the virus but it was impossible to know why it had hit her and not one of the rest of us. Later it would seem particularly devastating because, by the next spring (April, 1955), the polio vaccine developed by Dr. Jonas Salk had been licensed for use. My sister's case was one of the last reported ones in the Cincinnati area. She was paralyzed from the neck down and spent three months in the hospital in an iron lung respirator, a device that uses negative air pressure to help the paralyzed diaphragm to force air into the lungs to assist with breathing.

The cost of polio rehabilitation was more than the average family could afford, and more than 80 percent of the country's polio patients received funding through the March of Dimes. I remember, mostly through pictures and family stories, that Sylvia was a poster child for their fundraising for polio relief with the slogan, "Silver for Sylvia." A picture of her in the iron lung was flashed on television during station breaks.

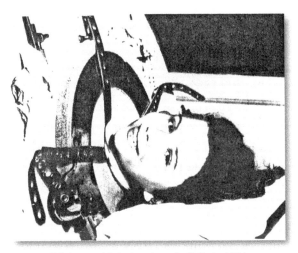

Sylvia, age 12, in iron lung for Polio in 1954.

In preparation for when Sylvia would be released from the hospital, some changes needed to be made to our small home. A ramp was installed at the back of the house for wheelchair access. And since the two children's bedrooms were on the second floor, our parents had to turn the dining room on the first floor into a bedroom for Sylvia. MaryLou and Sylvia had shared one bedroom and Nancy and I shared the other dormer. My parents spent many hours and much energy preparing for when Sylvia would be coming home.

After she was no longer dependent on the iron lung, Sylvia began rehabilitation at the Children's Convalescent Home. There she had therapy to learn how to walk with leg braces. Her left arm (which had been her dominant side) was completely paralyzed.

She underwent surgeries to improve the function of her non-dominant arm and had to learn how to do everything with that hand.

The polio virus took so much away from Sylvia at the young age of 12. She continued her schooling at the Children's Convalescent Home with other polio survivors until she was able to enroll in Seton High School for her junior and senior years. In spite of all of her challenges, she earned high honors and graduated with her class while defying the doctors who said that she would always be wheelchair dependent.

One of the best stories that I remember my mother telling about Sylvia in high school was that she received a demerit for running in the halls. Now that was a good one! She was lucky to walk occasionally at school, much less run. The only thing I can think of was maybe some of her classmates were running while pushing her in her wheelchair. Perhaps it was a case of guilt by association?

After high school, in order for her to gain more functional independence, Sylvia continued therapy for a year at the Georgia Warm Springs Foundation and through Goodwill Industries. The Georgia Warm Springs Foundation, now known as the Roosevelt Warm Springs Institute for Rehabilitation, was established by Franklin Roosevelt after he became convinced of the benefits of hydrotherapy and exercise while visiting a resort in the town known for its thermal springs. He subsequently purchased property there and established the facility for polio survivors to receive rehabilitation.

When the opportunity came for Sylvia to go to Warm Springs, we all piled into our 1954 Chevy with no air conditioning for the trip. We tried to make it seem like a family vacation, but unfortunately, because she was being evaluated and started on therapy and rehabilitation, Sylvia was not able to join in with us as we swam in the large pool there and enjoyed the novel experiences. The motel where we stayed was probably typical for the area in the 1950s. I remember that it was nothing fancy, just a small room where cockroaches ended up in our shoes overnight. My sister Nancy and I were particularly afraid of putting on our shoes and discovering a giant cockroach (or to use the polite term, palmetto bugs) in the toes. I also have memories of eating at a restaurant near the motel called "City Lunch" which we nicknamed "City Dump."

After Sylvia spent three months in therapy at Warm Springs, she worked for a year at Goodwill Industries. She was then admitted to a disabled students program at the University of Illinois. There she met other physically-challenged survivors whose motto was "...Ability, not disability, counts." She then went on to complete a master's degree in speech-language pathology at Southern Illinois University and subsequently set up the first hospital-based speech pathology department at Good Samaritan Hospital in Cincinnati.

I have memories from my early childhood of growing up the "baby" of the family of four girls. My older sisters always accused me of getting preferential treatment because of it. I loved having older sisters, but there was a pretty significant age difference between all of us.

My sisters, from top left: Nancy, Mary Lou, Sylvia and me.

MaryLou is the oldest. She was always very pretty and I remember boys hanging out at our house. She attracted many boyfriends and I even remember some riding horses over to our little house. I don't mean to make it sound like "Little House on the Prairie"—it wasn't that primitive! Looking back, I feel sorry for her position in the family because she had the pressure to go to work early to earn money for her own extras. She had many jobs in her teenage years working as a cashier in grocery stores and five and dime stores. After graduating from high school, she got a secretarial job at International Harvester. Even though she didn't have the opportunity to go college, she was able to find a good paying job.

Sylvia, named after our mother, was the next in the line. She was the sister who always did very well in school and, before she contracted polio, was a skilled roller skater who competed in contests and shows at our local roller rink. She was adorably cute, smart, talented, and very active in school activities.

Nancy is the third girl in the family and is probably the one I'm closest to because she was closest to my age. Five years separate the two of us. Don't get me wrong, I love having three older sisters, but there is a pretty significant age difference between MaryLou and Sylvia and myself, "the baby." Thirteen years separated MaryLou and myself and Sylvia and I were ten years apart. Nancy was one of the popular girls and was a cheerleader in grade school, whereas I was more of a tomboy and made all of the sports teams growing up. Nancy also said that she didn't get the opportunity to go to college after high school. She got a government secretarial job with the Marine Corps after working at Good Samaritan Hospital and as transcriptionist in radiology while in high school and for a while after graduation. Later in life, after moving many times as her husband climbed the corporate ladder, Nancy hung up her pom pom's, picked up a tennis racket, and became quite the tennis player and still plays regularly.

As for me, I decided to go to x-ray technology training after high school. I heard about the program from my sister Nancy while she was working as a medical transcriptionist in radiology. The program was offered through Good Samaritan Hospital and paid a small stipend while I earned the certificate that enabled me to take the state board that was necessary for becoming a registered radiologic technologist. After passing the boards, I secured a job at Good Samaritan Hospital where I trained and worked in the special procedures department. I loved my job, including Cath Lab and angiography cases. I always said that I hoped I would never have to be a patient on the neurology floor or that I would have any brain problems after having to put people through lumbar punctures, angiography, and pneumoencephalograms. Always be careful what you wish for!

Back in the days of x-ray before computed tomography (CT) scans and MRI studies, the way we had to image the brain was somewhat barbaric. The procedure was called pneumoencephalography to image the ventricles of a person's brain. We would have to strap a patient in a chair and the patient would be turned upside down, so we had to be sure we secured those straps correctly. The neurosurgeon or radiologist would do a spinal tap on the back of the patient through an opening in the back of the chair. Spinal fluid was drained from the ventricles and replaced with an injection of air that would enter the spinal canal and rise to the ventricles. This was done so the air in the ventricles would show up dark on the x-ray film in order to visualize them. The chair would be turned 360 degrees while the technologist's job was to take x-ray images in different positions. It was a very difficult procedure and many patients became quite nauseated during it.

As a young x-ray technologist I remember being scared to death when the chair was rotated wondering if I had secured those straps enough for us not to lose the patient on their head. You had to be quick and accurate when taking the films. The last thing you wanted to happen was a bad film from either the wrong exposure or incorrect positioning of the patient. In those days we would work as a team to have someone always with the patient, reassuring them and telling them to hang in there while the films were being processed. The patient would be upside down in an awkward position to allow the air to stay in the ventricles to be able to visualize them on the radiographs. We had automatic processors but still had to use the darkroom to unload the film manually in the dark and reload the cassette holder. The doctors would be outside the darkroom waiting a couple of minutes, which seemed like an eternity to the patient, to see if we obtained a diagnostic image. God help you if you messed up a film and a patient would have to take another spin in the awful chair! You would know immediately on opening the darkroom door if the neurosurgeon or radiologist was happy or not with your images. Lots of prayers were said in the darkroom in the special procedures department.

The invention of CT scans and MRI in the 1970s and 1980s has allowed radiologists to see so much more of the brain which makes neurological disorders easier to diagnose for both the patient and the doctor.

2

My Love, My Family, and Losing my Best Friend

In the early 1970s, while I was working at Good Samaritan in special procedures, a friend that I had trained with asked me to sing at her wedding. Actually this was not too unusual back then since I did play guitar and was told that I had a nice singing voice. After playing and singing at a couple of weddings, I became the "official wedding singer" for many of the technologists at the hospital. In fact, I also sang at graduation ceremonies, baptisms, funerals, you name it. I had a little side business going on while working as a radiologic technologist during the week and "flower child, church lady, guitar-playing singer" on weekends!

It was at one of these weddings that I was introduced to the man who would become my husband. We had hit it off at the reception, however, I didn't hear from him for a couple of weeks. When Dave finally called, I already had plans to leave for a weekend trip to visit my sister Nancy and her husband who had been transferred to Detroit.

He didn't give up though. Dave called when I returned and invited me to a formal dinner dance at the Hall of Mirrors, a grand ballroom in the Cincinnati Netherland Plaza hotel. We seemed to be drawn together, which was unusual for me. In high school, I was the girl who needed to be fixed up for dances and the prom. Somehow the dating scene passed me by while I was busy playing sports. I learned that Dave also had not dated much and when he did it was usually through someone setting him up with a sister. That fact that we both felt the attraction to each other was a different experience for us. I was an inexperienced 23-year-old and he was a very nice shy guy eight years older.

I had a trip planned at this time to go backpacking through Europe and Ireland with a friend that I had known since grade school. As Dave and I became closer and started to fall in love, I told him about my plans to explore Europe for 3 or 4 weeks. I had wanted to do this while I was single and didn't have a family to hold me back. Dave was fine with these plans and he took me and Kate to the airport in his mother's Cadillac with our backpacks, Earth shoes, jeans, and all!

It's surprising that my mother was okay with me taking this trip because she knew that we were so green and going abroad to unknown adventures. I was healing from a pilonidal cyst surgery on my tailbone and had been in the hospital for almost a week on my stomach in a bed with sheepskin pads cushioning my arms and with bandages on my tailbone that were changed daily. The incision was almost healed by the time we were leaving but the large backpack I would be carrying rested just above the incision area. By the way, Dave had come to visit me while I recovered from the surgery. Talk about embarrassing moments while dating!

I supposed the old saying, "Absence makes the heart grow fonder," is true because each time I sent a postcard to Dave while I was gone, the more I found myself missing him. Apparently he felt the same way. When we returned, he was there greeting us at the airport along with my parents and Kate's family. We had a fabulous time on our European adventure. It was a little scary at times, but I wouldn't have changed it for the world. What I must have put my parents through. I'm not sure that I would have wanted my daughter venturing off like that in today's world. It seems like maybe it would be more dangerous and risky. But maybe not. Maybe things aren't so different today.

After returning home, Dave and I were getting closer and started talking about getting married. But I wasn't quite ready. I had always wanted to move out of my parents' house and live in my own apartment. I convinced Dave that being out on my own and not going from living with my parents right into marriage was an important part of the process for me. After all, I was the "baby of the family," and I needed this as part of the growing process. It was at this time that I found out that a friend of mine from x-ray school was looking for a roommate to share the cost of an apartment, so she and I shared an apartment for a year. Dave and I got engaged and started planning our wedding which would take place in November, 1975.

God surely blessed me with my soulmate. What a wonderful husband and father to our children he blessed me with for 40 years of marriage. He was truly one of those good guys who turned out to be a diamond in the rough. We both blossomed from naive lovers to quite a team in marriage. We complemented each other as marriage partners. We both realized when the other needed space and were able to give up time together to allow each other to still have time with friends. He was the best and I feel so fortunate that we found each other. Truly a match made in heaven. Like so many couples, we had our share of ups and downs, but we always kept the faith and somehow ultimately came out stronger.

We were the parents of three wonderful children. Jennifer, our first, was born in 1977. It was a delight for both of us to have an adorable little girl. She was always strong willed and wouldn't take no for an answer. You will actually find out why her strong will is important for both of us later. She eventually followed me in the field of radiologic technology and became a CT and MRI technologist in Cincinnati. She's married, with a great husband, Nick, and two boys, Ian and Alex who are as smart and talented as they are handsome.

Christopher, our second, was born in 1979. He is a gentle, kind, and loving son. He is very much like his father in looks and actions. He's frugal and caring and is a good husband and provider. And in the tradition of his father, is an excellent cook, ice cream maker, and dad. He had a good role model. Chris received a bachelor's degree and then went on to get a master's degree in business. Chris married his beautiful wife Kara, and has two boys, Dawson and Zander. They are cute little guys who bring so much joy to my life.

Jeffrey, the baby, was born in 1981. He was our challenge and at times I thought he was allergic to school. Unfortunately, he had some physical problems from having undiagnosed, chronic mononucleosis. This led to migraine headaches in his early years of elementary school. They diagnosed him with ADD, but I suspect his attention issues were a result of his headaches. Lots of love and care went into getting Jeff through school with the benefit of homeschooling and family therapy to help him with his headaches and resulting fatigue and behavior issues. Jeff managed with help and understanding to make it through the rough patches and eventually become the family comedian and success he was destined to be. After high school, he completed the work for an associate's degree before going on to get a bachelor's.

We had a family friend who always told me not to worry about Jeff and that he would be a successful businessman some day and he has not disappointed. His sister Jennifer introduced him to a fellow radiologic technologist. It turned out that Jennifer was a good matchmaker. Jeff and Shelly were married on a beautiful snowy day and they have blessed us with three grandchildren, Charlie, Ava, and Myla.

My grandchildren on our family's vacation after Dave had passed.

Of all the trials we faced in our 40-year marriage, the hardest was when Dave found out that he had prostate cancer. Unlike many cases, his was a very fast growing invasive form that took us all by surprise. He was 69 years old and still working at the time, and we often talked about the trips that we would take after retirement. Unfortunately, those trips never happened because of this battle trying to outrun the fast spreading cancer. We were able to have one additional family vacation in Florida and a summer trip to Gatlinburg, Tennessee before the cancer really started to invade his spine, other bones, and brain before having to give up the fight in January and February, 2016. Dave entered hospice on February 19, 2016 after many of his cancerous bones had broken. He passed away just a few days later on February 21. The loss was very difficult for us all to grasp. Even though I thought that I was prepared, having spent so many days and nights at the nursing home with him, the reality of losing my first true love and soulmate was a shock both mentally and physically.

Dave and I with our children Jennifer, Christopher, and Jeffrey on one of our earlier beach vacations.

Fortunately, I had a great support system with all of my family living close by. In addition, my school friends had remained close and had been a great support throughout my life. Finally, with being involved with church music and liturgy for many years as a church music minister, I found God reaching out to me to get through. Without my faith, the grieving process would have been an extremely difficult task.

In the final weeks leading up to Dave's death, we were able to talk openly about what I was going to have to deal with on my own. One of our conversations that occurred when he realized that death was imminent took me by complete surprise. He told me that I should not hesitate to find someone else to have in my life after he was gone. I remember being so upset with him because I really believed, and still do, that he was irreplaceable. Surely I could never find another man like Dave, nor would I want to. We were a team! We loved everything about our married life and each other. He was truly one of the good guys in life and I know our children felt that same way.

3

Table for One: Transitions and Changes

S hortly after the loss and resulting pain of losing my husband, I sunk into a deep depression and was referred to a therapist in social work. I was having a very difficult time coping with the loss. At my son Chris' urging, I also participated in a six-week grief support group at a church while continuing to see the therapist. I had never done therapy before and always thought that I could handle anything life threw at me, but I found out that overcoming grief really threw me for a loop!

Except for taking family medical leave to care for Dave as we were losing the battle with cancer, I was still working part time at Good Samaritan Hospital. After Dave's death, I decided not to return to my high-pressure job and that I would take an early retirement. I was having trouble staying focused without the added stress of a job that included having to learn ever-changing technology. The passwords and computer skills that were important for doing my job were fading from my short term memory. And seeing so many patients deal with aging and illness made it even harder to concentrate and not relive the nightmare of watching my soulmate deal with his struggles of cancer and impending death. My heart and mind just were not in my job any longer. Therefore, I made up my mind that I needed to retire to try to heal from my grief and figure out where the road of my life without Dave would lead.

So, I was not only dealing with the loss of my husband, but also the loss of the social aspect of my job that had given me a feeling of self-worth. My social life outside of work was also completely transformed. When you become a widow, nobody really knows the empty and awkward feeling it is to socialize again with other married couples. That is until you have lived it. Nobody means to avoid you, it just happens.

I found myself feeling like a fifth wheel or not knowing what to do on weekends when people were busy socializing with other couples. I never wanted my kids to feel that they had to include me in their social lives, so I would try to have something to do. One thing that I would not do was to go to a restaurant and sit alone. But I found that drive-through restaurants were easier than cooking for myself at this time.

Just when I would think that I was doing okay, I would get a bad case of the blues and have a difficult time with depression and crying. Depression was affecting my life in other ways as well. I was always a person who liked to be busy shopping, socializing, and entertaining and just being active. But I was no longer getting enjoyment out of these things. It's funny how depression affects our life and moods. What used to give me great joy no longer had the same effect on my psyche. I was becoming a homebody and could not figure out where I fit in socially.

My family continued to be concerned about my condition. They wondered if I needed to see someone who could prescribe medication to help me feel less weepy and down. I didn't think the way I was handling my grief was that troublesome or unusual since we had been a happily married couple for 40 years and I didn't expect to get over it for quite some time, if ever. So I decided to continue meeting with my therapist and to see how things progressed.

Along with facing my grief and the changes in my social life, I had many other things to take care of after losing my partner of more than 40 years, such as getting finances in order and deciding whether to stay in the family home or downsize. As much as my family thought that they were giving me helpful advice about selling the house and moving to a smaller place, I felt that I needed to figure it out for myself. Living in my house brought me comfort at first, so I decided to stay put for a while.

While dealing with these issues, I started to realize that I was experiencing increasing moments of brain fog and forgetfulness that I often referred to as "brain farts". These episodes may have started prior to Dave's death, but because I was so consumed with being his caretaker and getting him to his appointments and therapies, that I may have been in denial about what was happening to me. During these episodes I experienced numbness in my face and arm and confusion in my thinking and memory. Convinced that I was experiencing ministrokes or transient ischemic attacks (TIAs), I ended up going to the emergency room several times to make sure that I was not mistaking an anxiety attack and was actually having a full-blown stroke.

My family, particularly my daughter, became increasingly concerned about these physical symptoms. Jennifer went with me to my primary care doctor to see if he had any ideas or recommendations regarding the symptoms I was experiencing. He referred me to the Christ Hospital Center for Health and Aging. Who me? I never had thought of myself getting old or possibly having dementia. They put in orders for a MRI of the brain before I had my first appointment and during the appointment, put me through a battery of cognitive tests used to detect dementia and

Alzheimer's disease. The MRI showed enlarged ventricles which can indicate brain atrophy due to injury or Alzheimer's disease. The cognitive tests showed some deficits in the ability to complete tasks and pointed to early dementia.

By the way, this was not the first time that I had been told that I had enlarged ventricles. Several years before, I had imaging done after another incident at work where a radiologic technologist pulled an x-ray tube down as I was coming up after positioning a patient and the tube and my head collided with considerable force. I literally saw stars and most likely had a concussion. I had a CAT scan the next day and the radiologist commented that my brain looked like the brain of an 80-year-old. He said that my ventricles were so big that my brain was shrinking because of the spinal fluid that filled the ventricles. The radiologist did not recommend any follow-up at that time, but just told me to be aware of any cognitive changes I might notice in the coming years.

The doctor from the Christ Hospital Center for Health and Aging recommended more physical activity and undergoing a sleep study since chronic sleep problems are associated with cognitive decline. However, my results showed just mild sleep apnea that did not require treatment.

The doctor also mentioned the possibility of starting on medication for dementia but said that they weren't having much success with it. In response to my daughter's concern about my potential for falling and about care that I might need in the future, the doctor recommended looking at nursing care facilities.

I decided not to start on any medication at that time, but did join a fitness center in an attempt to get more exercise and to socialize more. It started to become clear to me how much my balance was off during the classes that I participated in. I was struggling to follow the directions and to accomplish the task that should not have been a problem for a 68-year-old woman in a class with 80 and 90-year-olds. I was pathetic—definitely not the star pupil in the class!

During this time, I took a trip with my sister MaryLou and her husband to visit my sister Nancy and her husband in North Carolina. I tried to have a good time but the visit stirred up so many memories of when Dave and I would visit and we would need a table for six. Now we were five.

And my physical challenges seemed to become more noticeable. When my sisters and I would go for a walk to the beach, I was always the slow one trying to keep up. My sisters had a hard time understanding why I was so slow. I was blaming it on my previous knee replacement and the arthritic condition of my other knee. It eventually became more obvious that part of the problem was that I was having trouble with my right leg. It seemed to be dragging as I tried to keep up with my sisters' pace.

4

Seeking Help 2018

I continued to be concerned about the decline I was experiencing in my daily life. My daughter and I decided to look into second opinions from healthcare professionals. Jen was not convinced that what was happening to me was related to possible early dementia and she wanted to get another assessment.

We started with a neurologist at the UC Gardner Neuroscience Institute. I underwent a number of psychological and neurological tests to see what my memory and cognitive issues were and what might be causing them.

After already having been put through the battery of tests that detect Alzheimer's and other types of dementia at the Christ Hospital Health and Aging Center, I was getting pretty good at drawing the clock, counting backwards by sevens, and naming pictures of different animals. I don't know how many times I had taken the Montreal Cognitive Assessment test, but with trying to get other opinions, each provider would initiate their own set of tests. It was a real pain to go to different doctors only to have them not recognize that there was definitely an issue that needed to be addressed. But my strong-willed daughter was not going to give up on me though, and given that we are much alike in this regard, I was not going to give up on myself either!

With this appointment, I also had another MRI of my brain that showed enlarged ventricles. By this point, I was aware of the association between enlarged ventricles and NPH and that many of the symptoms that I was experiencing sounded like those describing NPH. During this time, I was having an increase in worrisome physical and cognitive issues. I had random falls, difficulty walking, forgetfulness, depression, difficulty handling my checkbook and paying bills, and loss of bladder control. I was feeling desperate to get someone to listen to me and figure out what was wrong.

The frustration of trying to get someone to come up with an answer was terrible! To me, it seemed pretty cut and dried that my symptoms fit the list of typical symptoms of Normal Pressure Hydrocephalus. I felt like I could be a poster child for the condition. Why were these neurologists not seeing what seemed so obvious to me and my family and friends?

Surely someone was going to see how bad I seemed to be deteriorating. Around this time, my girlfriends from high school had signed us up for a trivia night for alumni at our high school. We all met there and that particular night stands out to me as one where I was having a particularly difficult time walking and wondered, too, if I was still safe driving a car, especially at night. I must have had saints and angels watching over me that night, because I really struggled walking in when I arrived, but by the time the evening was over, trying to walk to my car was almost impossible! My friends walked with me to make sure I made it to my car. It was strange but my difficulty walking would fluctuate—at times I really struggled, but other times, it wasn't quite as bad. All I know is that night was one of the times that I was truly afraid! One of my friends who was a former physical therapist scared me that evening saying that my gait looked like that of a Parkinson's patient. "Oh great," I thought, now something else to worry about.

5

Meeting Ken, Fall 2019

So the elephant in the room was always there. When the family would gather, we all recognized that something was going wrong with me, but we continued to struggle to get a medical professional on board to come up with a diagnosis.

In early 2019 my sister Nancy, my daughter Jen, and I traveled to Las Vegas to visit my niece, her fiance, and her daughter. Since three of us have birthdays around the same time, we went to celebrate our birthdays there together. We had a wonderful time, and although we kept busy so that I didn't think much about it, I was slowing down in my walking and I had frequent incontinence problems.

Everyone was blaming my problems on depression and loneliness. So, while we were in Vegas, the younger girls ganged up on me and decided that I needed to get signed up with an online dating service. I was really against it because it just didn't seem right to me, but before I got back home, they had signed me up with a profile picture and such a storyline that I thought,

"Who wouldn't want to date me?" It was kind of fun and gave me something to do every day with checking for messages and responding to those who had reached out to me. I had a three-month introductory special and it helped the winter months pass quicker when we returned from our trip. It was kind of fun texting with some of the men and meeting some for a lunch or dinner date (in a public place), but I still was not that wild about putting myself out there to meet someone while wondering, in the back of my mind, about where this mystery illness was going and how bad I was going to become physically and mentally. I guess I really didn't want to get into a relationship and burden anyone with the problems that were starting to manifest themselves with more symptoms and more frequency.

In the fall of 2019, I was really having fun attending three of my grandsons' basketball games. I've always liked playing and watching sports, and now that my grandchildren were getting involved in sports, I enjoyed spending many hours in gymnasiums cheering them on and quite honestly probably making a fool of myself. I had fun being there as a fan and cheerleader, making it known what team and child I was cheering for.

One of the game days was a Saturday morning game. I was hurrying to get to the early game, when I took a bad tumble from the top step of my second floor and fell down all thirteen steps. Luckily I didn't break any bones, but I sure did scrape and bruise my body from the fall. I lay at the bottom of the staircase for what seemed like an eternity checking all the possible injured spots.

I knew that the fall down the stairs would have repercussions for me beyond my feeling sore and bruised. I knew that it was going to spur my family to start working on me to move from my home into a ranch or condo with all my living space on one floor. It made me start to feel vulnerable about getting older and dealing with balance issues. I must say that I was extremely lucky that I was only sore and embarrassed that I somehow slipped off the top step and couldn't do anything to stop the fall. Did you ever notice how it seems to feel like you're in slow motion when you are falling?

This is how much of a fan of the kids' sports that I am, I got up and went to the game! It was probably two or three days later that I realized how badly I had landed when all of the soreness, bruising, and aches and pains set in.

As a result of being at my grandsons' basketball games, I got to know my daughter's friends whose sons were on the team. My daughter and one of her friends had been talking about having me meet her mother's cousin at a game and then maybe going out to a local brewery for a drink. Ken and I were introduced while watching the game and then, at the brewery, we all sat together with the parents who had joined us. When the parents started leaving, Ken and I went outside by a nice moonlit lake behind the brewery, and we found it very easy to talk to each other. We wound up closing the place and then I drove him back to his car that was parked at the basketball complex up the road. We exchanged telephone numbers and vowed to celebrate Cincinnati's restaurant week together. I couldn't believe how well that blind date turned out for the both of us.

We have since dubbed September 13, 2019 the anniversary of our meeting! He seemed so worried about the almost ten year age difference between us, but I had been married for forty years to Dave with an eight year age difference. I guess you could say that I like older men!

So our relationship kind of took off that evening with us seeing each other, and as Ken put it, creating many firsts together. I couldn't help but think that Dave was happy that I met such a nice gentleman to be there for me, not realizing how much he was going to be needed in what was to come.

At first I wasn't exactly sure that my sons were on board with me dating someone. But I certainly knew that Jennifer was happy because she thought this was the answer to getting me out of the depression that she thought was causing my crying, confusion, falling, and overall sadness.

On the night we met, I told Ken that he might not want to get involved with me because I evidently had a problem and didn't want to drag him into my undiagnosed physical and psychological problems. His response to this was that he had problems that were going to have to be addressed too, so he understood. I guess you don't get to be sixty-eight and seventy-eight without having medical issues and other problems!

It was amazing to me that the Lord had a plan for our lives to come together where I could support Ken, and in turn, he could be helpful getting me through some upcoming really rough roads ahead on my journey to getting help. The Lord truly does work in mysterious ways.

Me and Ken at a Family Wedding

6

Normal Pressure Hydrocephalus Symptoms

W hen I started out writing this book, I had intended it to be something for my children to have as a memory of me and the medical issues I was experiencing after the death of their father. I can't tell you how many people encouraged me to get my story out there for others who might be dealing with issues like I had in the course of getting to a diagnosis and the eventual surgical procedure that kept me out of a memory care or nursing facility. It was what gave me "new life!"

As I said earlier, I was aware that my condition of enlarged ventricles in the brain was associated with NPH and as I read descriptions of the condition, I found that I was experiencing many of the symptoms. For those who may be wondering about those symptoms, here are the symptoms that Johns Hopkins lists on their website:

- Trouble walking (feels like feet are stuck to the ground)
- Poor balance
- Falling
- Changes in the way you walk
- Forgetfulness
- Mood changes
- Depression
- Difficulty responding to questions
- Loss of bladder control

Symptoms of adult onset hydrocephalus can include the following:

- Headaches
- Nausea
- Difficulty focusing the eyes
- Unsteady walk or gait
- Leg weakness
- Sudden falls
- Irritability
- Changes in personality and behavior
- Drowsiness
- Seizures

As the condition progresses some of the primary symptoms are:

- Gait disturbance and difficulty walking
- Dementia and forgetfulness
- Bladder control—Incontinence problems

Doctors said that an easy way to remember the primary symptoms is with the "three Ws—wet, wacky, and wobbly." As I said before, I could have been the poster girl for adult onset NPH!

The term hydrocephalus is derived from two words, "hydro" meaning water and "cephalus" referring to the head. It is a condition in which excess cerebrospinal fluid (CSF) builds up within the ventricles (the fluid containing cavities of the brain) and may increase pressure in the head. Hydrocephalus is sometimes described as "water on the brain," but the water is actually CSF, the clear fluid surrounding the brain and spinal cord. CSF has three functions:

- It acts as a shock absorber for the brain and spinal cord
- It acts as a vehicle for delivering nutrients to the brain and for removing waste
- It regulates pressure within the brain as it flows between the cranium and spine

The average adult produces about one pint of CSF daily. When an injury or illness alters the circulation of CSF, one or more of the ventricles enlarge as the fluid accumulates. As the ventricles enlarge, they can damage nearby brain tissue leading to the symptoms described above. In an adult the skull is rigid and does not expand, so the pressure in the brain may, but does not always, increase. In NPH, the pressure is normal.

Hydrocephalus is a chronic condition. It can be controlled, but usually not cured. With early treatment, many people can lead normal lives with few limitations. It can occur at any age but is most common in infants and adults over 60. Experts believe that NPH accounts for 5 to 6 percent of all dementia cases.

I was told by one physician that NPH can be a hereditary condition. That makes sense to me because my sister Sylvia had been diagnosed with it ten years before mine was discovered. At the time she was diagnosed, Sylvia's condition was too advanced and considered too risky for doctors to treat surgically. Continuing with the hereditary theory, my maternal grandmother was diagnosed in the late 1960s with dementia caused by "hardening of the arteries." Since this was prior to the advent of imaging studies through CT scan or MRI that would have shown enlarged fluid-filled ventricles, doctors were left calling forms of dementia that they saw in the aging and elderly population "hardening of the arteries." It is truly amazing what imaging improvements have opened up to doctors in modern times. Advanced imaging has allowed the brain to be seen in a new diagnostic light and has made it possible for neurosurgeons to treat NPH through the placement of a ventricular peritoneal (VP) shunt to drain the fluid.

7

Testing

W hile I continued to experience worsening symptoms, I tried to be proactive and take things into my own hands, and it helped to have a strong-willed daughter in the medical field. We had gotten a second opinion regarding the testing completed at the Christ Center by the neurologist at the UC Gardner Institute. And then saw another neurologist who did not have any further insight.

So my next step was to investigate some of the doctors' previous suggestions in regards to what could possibly be aggravating some of my goofiness or "wacky" episodes.

I had already completed the one sleep study at the Christ Hospital that indicated mild sleep apnea. One of the other neurologists discounted that test and ordered a second study which I completed at the UC Medical Center. The results of the second test were similar to the first, but the neurologist insisted that sleep apnea could be causing my brain fog and cognitive decline. I felt like I got fitted for a CPAP machine against my better judgment.

As a side note about the second sleep study, I question the validity of it because I went into it knowing that my daughter-in-law had gone into labor and was giving birth to my seventh grandchild while they were wiring me up and expecting me to sleep. Wonder why I struggled to get to sleep? I never really knew why the first study wasn't valid in the eyes of that neurologist. I actually slept better during the first test. After a night of not much restful sleep, I got up, showered, and tried to get the goop from the leads out of my hair. I proceeded to show up at the hospital to welcome baby Zander into the family. Hair goop and all! I looked like I had just been up all night giving birth!

I needed a lot of convincing to make me believe that a CPAP machine would be worth the investment and frustration of trying to sleep with it. I just had a very hard time believing that sleep apnea was the cause of my problems. But I got the machine only to have it be part of a large manufacturer's recall. Because of the size of the recall and because of Covid, the company has still not been able to replace all of the recalled units. I can't help but think that my apnea is not that severe. Pardon me for being a skeptic, but I start to wonder whether some of things are targeted to get seniors to fall for them. Don't get me wrong, if it was that bad, wouldn't you think that they would have insisted that I get a replacement right away?

The doctors had also encouraged me to get my hearing tested. I knew that I had been having hearing loss for some time. Even back when I was still working, when I had to go to the OR to take films, I had difficulty understanding the surgeons because I had relied on reading lips. That can be a difficult task when one is behind a mask! I had also been having trouble hearing the TV. When my kids came to my house, they all complained that I had the sound turned up too high. So now I'm wearing hearing aids in both ears, much to my family's and my delight. I will admit that it is good to be able to hear more of the conversation and dialogue in shows, at church, and while watching TV. That was one of the good things that came out of that test, $6000 later! It is really too bad that most insurance does not cover hearing aids, especially with the link to cognitive decline. Hopefully soon more plans will cover hearing aids. I can attest to the positive effect they have had on me to hear full conversations. Yet another advantage became apparent when we all began wearing masks to help stop the spread of Covid and my life became like my days in the OR when I couldn't depend on reading lips to help understand conversations.

So I am hearing better, supposed to be sleeping better (in spite of my faulty CPAP unit), but I'm still falling and my walking is deteriorating. I was starting to worry that we were missing something big here. My balance was getting worse even though I had joined the fitness center and was taking water exercise classes so that if I fell, I wouldn't hurt myself. Not only was my balance so bad that I couldn't really participate in the exercises, I had trouble comprehending the directions.

It's a good thing that I had a decent supplemental insurance plan, because between 2018 and 2022, I ended up having to undergo many tests and procedures. I had learned a very valuable lesson when Dave went through the cancer diagnosis and treatments. We had a good supplement then too. The last thing you want to worry about is cost when you feel like you're fighting to get your life back as you knew it.

At a previous appointment, the neurologist at UC had described that one way to determine if NPH is the cause of symptoms to determine whether a VP shunt might help is to perform a high volume spinal tap with an outpatient lumbar puncture. When I look back, I realize how lucky I was to have Jen with me for these appointments. She was my rock and a voice of concern for me. I signed off on an additional test where a sample of my spinal fluid would be sent to Boston to see if it contained markers for Alzheimer's disease. It scared me but I thought that if there was a chance that my deteriorating condition was caused by the early stages of Alzheimer's disease, I wanted to know. It was an extra part of the analysis and would be an extra cost out of pocket, but I wanted to know.

The lumbar puncture went well and large volumes of spinal fluid were collected. After lying flat for a while, I was able to get up and noticed an immediate improvement in my walking as I left the hospital. Jen and I were so excited because we were sure that this would convince the doctor that a shunt was worth trying.

Unfortunately the results of the evaluation for Alzheimer's markers was going to take 6 to 8 weeks. For me that was an eternity of waiting and stressing over whether I really wanted to know the results.

8

I Need a Break

S ometimes you can only take so much trying to get answers and second opinions when dealing with healthcare professionals. They just don't seem to be on the same planet with you. To me, it seemed so black and white as to what was changing my brain and balance and causing the "wet, wobbly, and wacky" symptoms that kept showing up so randomly.

It was during those eight weeks of waiting, that I decided to get on a plane with my sister MaryLou and her husband Jerry to take a break from all these tests, scans, and studies. We decided that we all needed a break. My sister Nancy understands so well how difficult it is to not let your mind go to places you'd rather not when waiting for medical results. She had invited us down to North Carolina for a visit. I had started questioning my decision to check for Alzheimer's markers. How would I react and handle news if it came back that I was declining because of that?

I don't exactly know why, but for me, being able to be near the ocean in a sunny spot and with some of my family seemed like the perfect prescription of "vitamin sea" for dealing with stress. And boy was I stressed! It was good to be on a break with my sisters, but we also felt sad that our sister Sylvia was having so many increasing mental issues and was unable to travel. Her life was pretty much having Henry, her dedicated husband, do everything for her. He would get her up, bathe her, dress her, feed her, and make her as comfortable as he could. There really aren't many husbands out there who would do what he did for my sister. For years we would suggest that he should consider putting her in a nursing facility. He would say that she probably would not have survived and would not have been taken care of as well as he did for her. He truly loved my sister and was an excellent caregiver for his wife of 50 plus years.

So this R and R was filled with fun and discussions about things like what I would do if the test of the spinal fluid came back positive for Alzheimer's markers. Would I really want to know or should I tell them that I would rather not know?

All in all it was a nice time. My friend Richard was scheduled to pick me up at the airport when I got home. MaryLou and Jerry had left ahead of me to get their luggage and pick up their car in the long-term parking lot. Because of my difficulty walking, I was not able to walk as fast as them and it took me a while to get to the baggage claim. While I was getting my luggage, I began to have a strange feeling in the right side of my face and my right arm was numb. The same feeling had happened before, and by the time I would get to an emergency room or a doctor's office, it would go away. Some doctors thought it was an anxiety attack but some said it was TIAs and I became too afraid to ignore them for fear of an impending stroke.

I found my luggage and called Richard in the cell phone lot to come get me. He asked me all kinds of questions about my trip, but I was struggling to make sense of this language and something just was not right. Thinking maybe I needed food, because I don't eat much when I fly, we went to one of our favorite Mexican restaurants that was on the way to my house.

The restaurant was short-lived because we hadn't ordered yet when Richard began to realize that something was going on. I was confused trying to answer questions about my trip, much less trying to order. I was still having tingling in my fingers, face, and arm. Richard called my daughter Jennifer and she told him to take me to the hospital emergency room that was closest to my house and she would meet us there.

I was admitted for two days of observation and tests. They did more brain imaging, and by now you can probably guess what the results were. I had fluid-enlarged ventricles and some infarcts, damaged areas, that were probably from some kind of head injury in the past. I was told to follow up with a cardiologist and get fitted for a Holter monitor to see if I had a heart rhythm problem. I had been there before, but here we go again.

Talk about frustration. Here I was returning home after a week away and all I wanted was to get back in my house and relax and I wind up as an inpatient for observation. I felt that they thought I was overreacting or making it up—that they thought it was "all in my head."

And my mind was racing with all kinds of thoughts of what I was possibly facing further down this path I was on. I didn't want my children to be faced with this burden, but reality was where this path was going to end and I was going to need a plan of action.

It wound up taking the full eight weeks or longer to get the results back from Boston. A conference was set up with my family and the neurologist around a large table for the presentation of the test findings. It was one of those good news/bad news moments. I wanted the good news first. The test did not show markers for Alzheimer's! Great news! However, the neurologist was not convinced that I could be helped with a shunt placement. Definitely bad news!

9

Taking on a Major Move—January 2020

S o at the end of 2019 I was feeling like I was running into a wall getting neurologists on board with my declining walking and those occasional episodes that were frightening to me.

I wondered if knee issues were contributing to some of my difficulty with walking and made an appointment with the orthopedic surgeon who had replaced my right knee in 2008. I had been told that my left knee was probably going to have the same fate at some point. I was feeling fortunate that I had delayed the inevitable for so long, because 12 years prior, the left knee really wasn't looking good with bone on bone. Retirement probably helped since I wasn't on my feet on those hard floors at work. I also wondered if, because I had a bad left knee, I was making the replaced right knee work too hard and that was causing the weakness and drag I was experiencing in my right leg. I truly was groping for reasons for my right leg "shuffling."

I must admit that I was a little afraid of going under anesthesia because of the mental fog that accompanied the episodes that I was having. But because things actually seemed to be going okay at the start of 2020, I decided to go ahead with the left knee replacement. I felt that it was worth a try to see if maybe a new knee might help improve my gait and decrease my falls.

I had finally decided to sell my home in the summer of 2019 and had purchased a condo not far away. I was able to accept an offer on my house the second day on the market in a bidding war with four offers on the table. I was excited to get such a great offer, only to be disappointed by the buyer backing out the day before closing. The other bids were close to hers, but I didn't know at the time that this would happen. I had even extended the closing date for the buyer with not much promise money from her to protect me from something like this happening. I learned a hard lesson from that! After putting it back on the market, I wondered if people would be afraid to come in again and the others who were interested had moved on to other properties. My house was located in a great school district in a desirable neighborhood, but, by the time I got it back on the market, it was too late for those families wanting to move before school started in the fall. I learned from this that timing is everything! I was able to sell again and closed by the end of 2019 after taking a big cut in the final offer compared to the first one. I then updated and painted my condo and moved in during the first week of January 2020.

My move turned out to be a good one with my upcoming knee replacement because everything I needed would be on one floor. Ken (my new friend) offered to come and stay with me and help me through the rehabilitation after the surgery.

My daughter insisted that I plan to go to a rehab facility the first week or so to get back on my feet before going home. The surgery was on March 4, 2020. Everything went well with the surgery and I was doing great with therapy, until the pandemic arrived here in Cincinnati shutting down visitation at the rehab facility. I felt like I was learning what it would be like to be all alone as a resident in a nursing home. My first few days I was able to have visitors, but eventually no one was allowed in. I had my mind made up that I was going to work hard to get my knee bending and get home to continue with home therapy. At one point a friend came and visited outside my window and we communicated to each other by telephone. The pandemic was just starting and it was frightening.

Kate's photo of me "waiting by the window" at rehab during Covid visitor restrictions.

The days in the rehab weren't so bad since I was occupied with physical and occupational therapy, but the nights were awful. Being stuck so to speak in a nursing rehab facility with the average age being 80 plus, I was the "new kid" on the floor at 68. Little did these people know, but I was also having brain issues that were starting to surface again after the anesthesia for my surgery. I'm not sure that this had anything to do with it, but my post surgery rehab success was short-lived. I couldn't wait to get home and get a good night's sleep. The nights were a whole different game especially in a Covid pandemic. The staff was decreased and my buzzing for help to use the bathroom and trying to get help with showering was often too much to ask of an overworked skeleton staff. My heart went out to all the elderly patients who were not able to get out of their beds, much less their rooms. I would visit them from my wheelchair at their doorways and converse with them to pass the time. It was a very sad time for so many of the really old people. They seemed to be stuck in the facility with really difficult rehabilitation that they were facing without much of a chance of getting to go home. This had become their home and family members were no longer allowed in to visit due to the Covid restrictions. It was a horrible time for these people who had to be feeling like they were forgotten. There were some tough long nights where I lay awake listening to the cries of those lonely elderly patients calling out for help and their families. Sleeping pills became a necessity for me to get a decent night's sleep in order to work hard at therapy the next day. It was truly a sad situation when Covid hit.

10

Covid Pandemic Arrives

Well I made it through the total knee replacement and the rehab nursing facility in what was the beginning of the Covid pandemic. The knee replacement and results were a piece of cake compared to what I was about to face in 2020.

News of the spreading pandemic was the focus on everyone's mind after its arrival in March 2020. Once I returned home, physical therapy, occupational therapy, and the home health nurse visits took up a big part of my days. I started losing ground on the rehab part of this whole process after about the fifth week. Ken was staying with me, and on the days that the weather was nice enough, he would help me practice walking in the parking lot across from my condo. The hills in my neighborhood were sometimes too much for me. It really wasn't so much because of the left leg and the replaced knee as it was that my right leg seemed to not want to pick up and was dragging along the pavement. It didn't feel weak, it would just feel stuck or like I couldn't pick up my foot. My shoes were wearing out from dragging along the pavement.

With the pandemic, came doctor appointments conducted online with Zoom and FaceTime. Thank God I had children who were able to come help me figure out how to do this. I'm not sure that I really ever did figure it out, but was able to manage with their help.

I can't explain the frustration I was having trying to get an answer to what I was experiencing in my day to day life. I never knew which day I was going to wake up and deal with walking issues, falling, mental fog, and incontinence issues. And I had gotten so used to waking up with headaches that I had quit complaining about them long ago. My knee replacement was doing fine, but I felt like nobody really understood that terrible time I was having trying to get help for the other issues.

After it was no longer necessary for Ken to stay with me, we decided that he should return to his house. We would communicate by phone and visits so that he could get back to his lifestyle and I could start to become independent in my new home. Home health supplied me with an "I've fallen and I can't get up" alarm which helped with my fear of falling in my shower and being alone. I put that call button around my neck and felt better knowing that I was somewhat safer if, God forbid, I would need to use it!

11

Rehab Only to Relapse

I was pleased with the initial progress with all the home healthcare workers who came for my therapy. The nurse who came was wonderful. She was confused by the stories I shared with her about all the neurologists I had been to prior to my knee replacement trying to get an answer to the walking, falling, and mental issues I was experiencing prior to my surgery.

Even though the knee is healing properly, I kind of hit a wall with the progress at week five post surgery. The replaced knee was healing fine and looking good, but my balance and my right foot drag was soon to become my next issue. I just wasn't feeling as sharp as I had been those first weeks after surgery.

After the home healthcare services ran out and I was released from therapy, I was on my own, with the help of Ken, to continue doing my exercises and work on balance issues. The only problem was I could have worked on balance until the cows came home, but with fluid collecting in my ventricles, I now know that I would have never succeeded.

Between Covid precautions and travel restrictions, and not getting any younger, we did what any crazy-minded people would do after getting vaccinated against Covid, we scheduled a trip to North Carolina to visit my sister Nancy!

My sister MaryLou and her husband had already planned on being there when Nancy suggested that Ken and I make the trip to celebrate my new left knee. Ken was excited to travel and visit their home in Wrightsville Beach, North Carolina since he had never been there. Ken and I did a lot of FaceTime on the phone with Nancy when I was recovering from surgery and I really wanted Nancy and Tony to get to meet Ken in person and get to know each other better.

I was extremely fortunate that even though I was having all these issues, I was still able to travel with Ken's help. I don't think I would have been up for trying any of these trips alone for fear of having one of these random episodes happen. We had a very enjoyable trip and my family was happy to meet Ken, my new best friend and the guardian angel looking out for me. I had found out that it's very important to have an advocate to help when dealing with medical issues.

We made it through this trip without a hitch, only to have things change and start up again on returning home. Around this time, I was having increased memory lapses, brain fog, and occasional facial numbness, making me wonder if it was a TIA or a ministroke. I had a dental appointment in the midst of all this going on and Ken had taken me to the appointment. He was not allowed to go in with me due to Covid precautions, so he waited in his car while I had my teeth cleaned. I'm not sure what happened, but I was so frightened because I evidently had a brain episode. I was trying to communicate with the hygienist but she couldn't understand or make sense of what I was trying to communicate. They asked me for Ken's telephone number so that they could have him come in but I was unable to communicate. One of the staff was able to find him in the parking lot and they had me come to the front entrance to pick me up and take me home. Looking back I'm not sure that was a very professional way to handle this situation. I just knew I was so pathetically scared that I just wanted out of the office and wanted normalcy to return.

My home health nurse was scheduled to come that afternoon already and was on her way to meet us at my condo. After hearing what had just happened at the dentist's office, she checked my vitals and asked me questions. She was not feeling good about how I was answering questions about what had happened and she called the life squad to take me to the hospital. I was taken to the emergency room, but, by the time we got there, many of my symptoms had subsided. So yet another false alarm in this long journey of episodes on the road to getting help.

You can only imagine how frightening this condition of brain fog and stroke-like symptoms were becoming. I needed someone to find the cause of these continuing issues. All the tests that were run in the emergency room were not showing anything different from previous studies. I was eventually discharged, only to go home wondering what had happened to me once again that day. All I know is each time this happened, I was getting more and more apprehensive as to when a major event might occur. It was very scary not knowing what was causing my issues.

As my walking continued to deteriorate, Ken had the idea of taking a video of me. We were going to watch my grandson's baseball game. After we arrived and saw how far away the field was, I decided to use my walker. The longer I would have to walk, the worse my ability became to do it without using a walker for assistance. Ken thought that the video would be a good way to show the neurologist how bad my walking was becoming when I had to go very far. What a great idea he had so that we could let them see what we were talking about! That particular video was very valuable and got the attention the next time I was admitted. It actually scared me to see how bad I had gotten in such a short time. Something was definitely going wrong here!

12

Blitz Hits

As had happened before, I had a little lull in anything scary happening for about three or four weeks. But Ken had taken over doing the driving for me for fear that I would have an episode while I was behind the wheel. I had actually experienced a couple of episodes while driving. I really didn't want to give up on driving, but my family was getting concerned about the safety issue of me getting confused and lost. On one particular day, Ken and I drove to Costco to stock up on some things I needed. When we arrived, I was feeling fine and we decided to shop for wine and liquor first since it was in the front of the store. I needed some gin for my summertime drink of choice—gin and tonic. While looking around, I started to feel a rush of anxiety creeping over me. I thought I was going to pass out and felt an impending doom coming over me. I turned to Ken and told him that something was wrong with me. It seemed like a classic panic attack until I sat down to wait for Ken to go get the car. By the time he returned, I was having a difficult time understanding what was going on around me and needed assistance to get out the door and into the car. An employee came to help because I was unable to cooperate and follow directions, much less bend my legs to allow myself to be seated in the car.

Ken put in a call for Jennifer because he wasn't exactly sure what he should do since I wasn't responding very well. I was scared because I was sure that this was what it was like to be having a stroke. I was weeping like a helpless baby. Poor Ken was so scared but stayed calm enough to drive me to the emergency room at UC Medical Center Hospital where Jen had encouraged him to take me.

Once we arrived at the emergency room, it took several people to get me out of the car and into a wheelchair. I was in and out of awareness of what was happening, but I remember some of the events. Once in the ER, I was placed on a stretcher and a team of doctors and nurses were all over asking questions and starting IVs. I was trying to process what was taking place. I didn't know what the heck was happening but knew it wasn't good. The ER was pretty crowded and I remember that my stretcher was up against the wall. I was so confused as to what got me in this predicament. I remember being so scared as I listened to doctors talking to patients on either side of me. They were discussing spinal taps with another patient who seemed to be confused like I was.

The hospital was pretty full with Covid cases and it seemed like once they ran the usual work up tests and decided to admit me for evaluation, there were no rooms available. That meant staying in the corner of the ER on a stretcher most of the night until a room became available.

I was getting used to having these episodes and it seemed like they were picking up more and more since my knee replacement in March. This particular one seemed to be the worst so far. I was really thrown for a loop mentally. After spending the night in the ER they finally got me a bed in the old part of the hospital that

I believe they said was being used during Covid as a holding area until a bed became available on the neurology floor.

Later in the morning rounds started and in march the attending neurologist and a staff of residents and interns. I was a puzzling case for everyone. I'm not sure my symptoms were necessarily the typical ones that they were used to seeing with an NPH diagnosis. The wacky part of my wet, wobbly, and wacky symptoms was getting very wacky. I was so confused this time in the hospital that I thought Jen had arranged a surprise party for me. In my mind, the staff was becoming people I knew coming to visit and surprise me. When a staff member would come in, I would ask them if they were in on the surprise. When Jennifer called, I asked her how she had set this all up and had arranged to have so many of these people I thought I knew get in to visit me since during Covid restrictions, only one family member could visit per day. My actual visitors—my sons Christopher and Jeff, Jennifer, and Ken were taking turns being my designated visitors.

I definitely needed an advocate with me because of the hallucinations that I was experiencing. I was not very good at remembering who was coming in to see me. To me it was just a big surprise party! Looking back, I can see that I was really wacky this time. I felt like the day was something I had dreamed or lived through before. The room, the surroundings, and the people all seemed way too familiar to me. As Jennifer put it, I had made things easier for the family to go through this experience because I was happy those first few days thinking it was a party for me!

One funny incident that I remember about this hospital stay seemed to be a memory of mine from a dream or hallucination. The older part of the hospital was staffed with UC nursing students as aids. When I would buzz for help to the bathroom, usually two students were sent together to get me up. I was considered a "fall risk" because of the upswing of falls I was experiencing. The call system in this part of the hospital was an old antiquated system. I wasn't wearing my hearing aids while in bed, so when

I would buzz I was confused to always hear, "The canteen has been thrown." I would wonder, time after time, why they would say such a thing. I finally asked one of the students that showed up why they would throw a canteen. It took them some time to figure out that I was asking about what they actually were saying, which was, "The care team has been called." I believe they thought I really was losing my mind and looked at me as such! I explained that's what I thought I was hearing over the speaker in my room. We all had a good laugh over that one and I found out why I was thankful for my hearing aids. Being hard of hearing can really affect cognitive impairment. I get it now! I was getting so confused. Kudos to the neurologist who had me get my hearing tested. I found that I had been missing and misinterpreting so much sound and conversation with my significant hearing loss. I'm still not sure how I interpreted the word "called" as "thrown." However, I do understand my confusing "canteen" and "care team." That I totally understand.

One of the first tests that they conducted was a continuous EEG. I was wired up like I was an alien from another planet. I thought the overnight sleep study goop in the hair was bad until I had this test done. Once again, this machine looked like some antique piece of equipment and I couldn't help but wonder what they could tell from this test.

It seemed like with all of the suggestions by the doctors and residents, it always came back that they thought an inpatient lumbar drain should be done to see if there was a vast improvement in my gait, cognition, and overall awareness of what was happening when I had these wet, wobbly, and wacky episodes. My family and I were pushing to get this done sooner rather than later since I was already an inpatient. Instead the doctors talked about dismissing me and sending me home.

This is where that strong-willed advocate of mine, my daughter, became the voice I needed to demand that I not be sent home. She said that I was in no condition to be released at this stage. At one point in this long process of trying to get help, I was told of a renowned doctor, Dr. Espay, at the UC Gardner Neuroscience Institute who worked with motion disorders and Parkinson's disease patients. I had previously called and made an appointment with him when seeking second opinions. It was very difficult to get in to see him and my appointment was scheduled for eight months in advance, in the fall of 2020.

We continued to push for the continuous drain spinal tap to happen while I was a patient to no avail. There was a fourth-year resident who took my case seriously who told me and Jen that she agreed that I should not go home from the hospital directly without going to rehabilitation first. She was going to get that in place and was going to set up an appointment with Dr. Espay in two to three weeks. If it wasn't for her, I'm not sure how much longer I could have waited to get help.

13

Getting Support and the Neuro Team on Board

A fter this rather long hospital stay, I was set up to go to rehab at a facility close to home. Because of Covid restrictions, my visitors were limited and my support team of Ken, Jennifer, Chris, and Jeff were my faithful visitors. The visitation rules were the same as at the hospital, one person per day. The care and rehabilitation team was very good at working to get me back on my feet and helping me with being able to show that I could return home safely on my own. The physical, occupational, and speech therapists made sure that I had ways to get up from the floor if I fell, that I knew how to use my cell phone to get help, and made sure that I had an alert call button to wear while in my house.

Prior to getting the button, I had been experiencing quite a lot of falls. Many of them happened when I was alone at home at night or in the early morning. Several times while I was sitting on the edge of my bed, I would slide off and wind up on the floor. This was not a good thing because due to my latest knee replacement and the previous one, I had a heck of a time rolling around on the floor trying to find something to pull myself up with. I remember falling asleep on the bedroom floor a couple of times because I couldn't figure out a way to get up or because I was just too pooped out and had no strength to pull myself up.

One of my earlier falls was in the bathroom after a shower. Talk about embarrassing! I was able to yell for Ken who was staying with me during my rehab from the knee replacement. He was unable to help me up from the floor alone and was afraid that he might hurt both of us, so he called my son Jeff who lived the closest to me. Ken got me a towel to cover up with while we waited for Jeff to come. How embarrassing!

Yet another bad fall was in my kitchen when I fell from a counter height chair while getting onto it. That particular fall was a really bad one with me falling headfirst into the corner of the wall. I was left with a big bruise on my forehead and a black eye!

The fall that was probably the scariest and most embarrassing was outside in front of my condo in early summer. I enjoy working in the yard and garden but hadn't been able to do much because of my knee rehab. One day I decided that I could work in my cute little fenced-in garden area in front of my condo. I had planted some flowers in the window boxes and was bending over to turn on the hose when I lost my balance and fell headfirst into some bushes. At first I tried yelling for help. I noticed an elderly man walking a dog past my place but he didn't hear me. Because my yard is at a lower elevation than the sidewalk, apparently no one could hear my cries for help. I tried numerous times to get myself up and out of the prickly bushes only to keep scratching my face and arm. I was unable to fully use my knee yet to help me extricate myself from the bushes. I kept hollering uselessly for help but then thought of my alert button. It was supposed to work mainly inside the house but I thought, "What do I have to lose?"

I started pushing that button multiple times! I didn't know how long I had been stuck there and didn't know if the button would actually work. Occasionally I would try to reposition myself only to scrape up my skin even more and still had no luck in pushing myself up enough to get my head out of the bushes.

So here's a visual: have you ever seen at Halloween those legs with orange and black striped hose and red glittery shoes sticking out of a bush to look like the wicked witch landed headfirst into the bush? There you have it. However my legs didn't have the cute socks and shoes, just bare legs with bloody scratches.

A visual representation of my head-first fall into my condo's bushes.

Just when I was about to give up calling for help, I heard a siren in the distance. Could it be that my alert button actually worked? The siren was getting louder and I realized a truck was up on the street outside my home. They had sent a hook and ladder fire truck and an ambulance with many fire personnel. I was so happy yet embarrassed to be found in such a predicament.

The fire chief told me that at first they didn't see me when they pulled up. That may explain why the elderly man with his dog missed me too!

The firemen found a folding chair in my garage and they pulled me up and out of the bushes and sat me in the chair. One of the paramedics looked over the cuts and scratches and asked if I wanted the squad to take me to the emergency room. He also asked how I managed to get in this predicament. I explained that I had a neurological problem that was causing balance issues and that I was experiencing many falls and that this one happened while I was reaching for the faucet to turn on my hose.

I actually had an appointment to see Dr. Espay, the neurologist at UC Gardner Neurological Institute, that afternoon. When I realized that all I had were scrapes, cuts, and bruises, I decided to just get cleaned up and keep the appointment that was so hard to get. I was also thinking what better story to relay to the doctor to illustrate the issues I was having. Wacky and wobbly, right?

So I kept my appointment with the neurologist and ended up with a whole team made up of the neurologist, psychologist, psychiatrist, neurosurgeon, and others who were involved in testing me to see if I would benefit and qualify for a VP shunt. I would undergo more CT scans, MRIs, psychological tests, a video walking test, and finally the continuous lumbar drain during an inpatient hospital stay.

I finally felt that I was in the right place to get the help I needed at this appointment with Dr. Alberto Espay and his team. It was after my exam with him and after a quite lengthy evaluation that he said the words I had been longing to hear. He looked right at me and said, "I believe we will be able to help you." Tears flooded my eyes as I felt that this long journey of trying to figure out what was wrong with me may finally get solved.

Dr. Espay referred me to Dr. Juan Torres, a neurosurgeon who ultimately would be performing the surgery to place the VP shunt if the team gave me the go ahead. It wasn't going to be easy or cut and dried without first getting scheduled for a consultation with Dr. Torres and more tests to prove that I was going to be mentally and physically ready for this type of brain surgery. Even though it was not considered that high risk, it did come with potential risks that they wanted to be sure I was aware of. I also would need more imaging tests, psychiatric evaluation, and cognitive evaluations before and after the high-volume continuous spinal fluid drain during a five-day hospital stay.

It was such a good feeling to finally get a team on board and to realize that it wasn't just "all in my head." I really did have a medical condition that Dr. Espay believed could be treated.

14

Head Blows Take a Toll

A ll I could think of was "please let's get this going before I have a really bad fall and it's too late to fix my issues" much like what happened with my sister Sylvia. The doctors did not see the value in a VP shunt for her wacky issues. I still feel that maybe the placement of a shunt could have possibly made an impact on her mental status and that she and her husband may have been able to communicate better those last ten years of her life. She had had many falls in her life after polio and had hit her head and face because she was unable to stop the fall from happening when she lost her balance. Later in life as falls increased, she had humerus fractures, leg fractures, and multiple head hits that probably didn't help the NPH that she also demonstrated on MRIs. We didn't expect the miracle of her walking again, but it would have been nice to see if her mental status could have been improved over time by draining the excess fluid from her ventricles. My sister was a very intelligent woman and an accomplished speech pathologist who, even with her severe handicaps, was able to become a respected professional in her field. Her first job was to establish the speech therapy department at Good Samaritan Hospital in Cincinnati after she earned her Master's degree in speech and hearing at Southern Illinois University.

She worked with many patients who had suffered strokes, patients with closed head injuries, and patients with aphasia. One of her patients was a very well known professional basketball player for the Cincinnati Royals – Maurice Stokes. In 1958, he suffered from post-traumatic encephalopathy, a brain injury attributed to an collison and fall on the court that caused a seizure and paralysis. Part of the therapy sessions that my sister had with him consisted of him dictating to her things about this life that he would like to have written as a memoir. I was in high school at the time and Sylvia would have me practice my typing skills by transcribing her notes from what Maurice communicated to her in therapy. It was mostly for Maurice to practice his speech in his therapy sessions. I recently came across those pages that I had typed and found it quite interesting to re-read them. At times he related memories he had of his college days at St. Francis University where he played collegiate basketball prior to his short-lived professional career. Other days he shared his philosophical observations of life, including what he saw from the window of his hospital room.

Sylvia and Maurice formed a wonderful friendship because they both knew what it was like to have been living a very normal life before becoming paralyzed. I'm sure my sister was an inspiration to many people seeing how much she was able to overcome in her life.

Maurice was a very big man and the hospital had a special large room that became his new home. Jack Twyman, a team member and friend, was his legal guardian. He made sure that Maurice was well-cared for. With Maurice living at the hospital, he could receive physical, occupational, and speech therapy on a regular basis. Maurice was a star and people enjoyed being around the infectious good moods he displayed in spite of the hardships he had to bear for the rest of his life after being robbed of the use of his arms and legs, his basketball talents, and his speech. What a sad outcome for him in his prime of life.

It is interesting to me that my sister had worked with so many patients who were affected by brain injuries and other conditions and then was diagnosed herself with a brain condition that had devastating effects. In seeing what happened to Sylvia and in hearing about my grandmother's early "hardening of the arteries," I'm very grateful that I've been able to get help. I really do believe that my symptoms became more pronounced after that scary evening at work when I had a blow to my head. That was when I first became aware that I had extremely large ventricles and seemed to begin to have symptoms that eventually could have made me a "poster child" for NPH! In hindsight, I think my work performance was declining at that time. But because I was so absorbed with my husband's cancer diagnosis that I didn't realize that I was on a mental and physical decline myself.

15

High Volume Spinal Tap

(Inpatient Continuous Drain)

L ooking back on this journey to get help, I can't help but remember how scared I was when I went in for the first high-volume spinal tap as an outpatient to determine if I could possibly be helped by the placement of a VP shunt. I vividly remember Jennifer and I had been so excited about the outcome that day when I got off the table and felt so much more in control of my walking out of the medical office building that day!

We had gone to lunch and talked about the possibilities of getting people on board to see that a shunt was going to be what I needed to help my issues of wet, wacky, and wobbly. I was to keep a personal journal to see how many days I felt like I was seeing improvement in my walking, incontinence issues, mental fog, and so on, until the ventricles filled with fluid again.

I remembered the great disappointment I felt when I was told by the first neurologist that he did not think I would benefit from a shunt placement. It seemed so black and white to me and my family that I would be a candidate for the surgery. The fluid that was tested did not show Alzheimer's markers. Remember that was the good news, but yet we still had a physician telling us to go check out nursing facilities to deal with my declining mental status. As I said previously, I wonder how many people might be spending their days in nursing homes who may have been helped with the placement of a VP shunt. In the time since I was diagnosed with NPH, this once little-known condition is finally getting more and more recognition.

Dr. Torres explained to me the steps that would need to be completed before scheduling the surgery. First there were more MRIs and PET scans and, finally, the very important hospital admission for the continuous lumbar drain. The continuous lumbar drain, where a thin flexible tube is surgically placed in the lumbar spine region took place the first week of November, 2020. I was hospitalized for five days while cerebral spinal fluid was drained, collected, and measured around the clock. After the drain was removed, I immediately went through the same cognitive psychological tests and a walking test to see if I demonstrated improvement in order to qualify for the placement of the VP shunt.

Next, armed with the information gathered from all of the tests that had been conducted before and after the lumbar drain, the doctors who were involved would have a conference to present their input as to whether we should proceed with the surgery.

At my next appointment with Dr. Torres, after all the data and results were collected and reviewed by the neuro team, he came in smiling and told me that I qualified for the surgery! Next, the scheduling nurse came in to describe potential risks and for me to sign paperwork. I was so ready by this point to take on any potential risks of brain surgery for a chance to return to the life I was living before all of the symptoms of NPH struck. All I could think of was that I had to take a chance because the life I was living was not where I wanted to be.

It was finally happening! I was scheduled for surgery on December 4, 2020. I continued to meet with the psychologist to talk about handling any fears I had about the upcoming surgery. It's funny that the things I was fearful of, were in hindsight, so insignificant after all I had been through getting to this point. I just kept thinking about how Dr. Torres explained that this type of procedure was not that dangerous, but because it was brain surgery and comes with risks, patients need to be made aware prior to consent.

My two main fears were that of secondary infection and post-surgical bleed along with going through the surgery and not seeing improvement. One of the more insignificant concerns many of us vain women may relate to was, whether they would shave my whole head. I had always been complimented on my good thick head of hair, and like so many women, I foresaw myself as perhaps having to wear a wig or a hat for some time post surgery. Then I thought about so many friends and family members who have dealt with hair loss from chemotherapy and radiation treatments or from alopecia. That thought put this worry into perspective for me. These issues and fears eventually take care of themselves in due time with regrowth or learning to love yourself just the way you are.

16

Starting to See an End in Sight

After spending the better part of 2020 working through so many ups and downs, first with rehabbing my new knee and then with escalating NPH symptoms, it was a very eventful year for me! My family and Ken were my rocks who believed that we were going to get to the bottom of all these strange symptoms that I was experiencing.

Now, here I was finding myself closing in on my scheduled day for the surgery hopefully going to change my life for the better. Then, I was notified that the surgery that was scheduled for December 4 was canceled, because of a rise in Covid cases. All elective surgeries needed to be rescheduled. You can only imagine the disappointment I felt not knowing how long it would have to be put off.

I was shopping at the grocery store when I took a call from UC Medical Center breaking the news to me that we needed to hold off rescheduling indefinitely. I had myself so ready to have the surgery only to have it delayed just days before the scheduled date.

I was so depressed that I decided to go looking for a new car that weekend so that, after surgery, when I could drive again, I would have a car with a backup camera. My condo's driveway is quite a hill that slopes down to the garage. The visibility while backing out was limited. I had really cut back on my driving due to fear of the episodes that I was experiencing that had taken me to the emergency room so many times in 2020. I decided a new car would give me incentive to recover faster once I had the shunt placed. I figured that if things didn't work out so that I could drive again, I could always sell the car or give it to a family member.

I ended up purchasing a small SUV that I fell in love with at the dealer. Thinking that I probably wasn't going to get my surgery rescheduled until 2021, I bought the car as an early Christmas gift to myself for the rough 2020 I had experienced. Talk about wacky, but funny what some will do when they are feeling down. I guess most "normal" people would have gone on a shopping spree for new clothes or something you could return easier than a new car!

However, there was really nothing "normal" about this girl with Normal Pressure Hydrocephalus!

17

Surgery is Back On!

I nterestingly enough, the delay for my surgery was only about one week. When the nurse called to cancel the December 4th date, I had no idea she would be able to get me in a week later on December 11th. I think it surprised her too because she was juggling so many schedules. It was not an easy task to coordinate and manage all of the moving pieces—the hospital staff which was dealing with the rising Covid cases, the neurosurgeon's schedule, the general surgeon's schedule, and an OR schedule that included many surgeries.

The scheduler knew how disappointed I was when she had to cancel the initial date. The disappointment was hard to hide in my voice because I was so prepared and ready to get it done. She was probably surprised and happy to be able to call me a short time later to make me aware that things had opened up rather quickly. So the date was set for December 11.

God truly is good! I felt so blessed that I didn't have to wait until 2021 to get the surgery done. Waiting and wondering, worrying, and getting anxious were always a fault of mine, I must admit. If I learned anything in this journey, I learned the power of prayer and waiting for God's time. So many people were praying for me and sincerely wishing for the best outcome from my shunt placement. I was concerned about going under anesthesia again and wondering how I would feel when I woke up. Would I notice a difference right away? Would it take some time before my issues would improve? How long would it take for my shaved head to grow back? (Yes, that was a concern for me!)

Looking back on my life that morning of my surgery, I was so calm and ready. I'm sure the Lord had his hand in leading me to this place, this date, these surgeons, and this staff. All that was left for me to do was trust. When I was a young x-ray technologist, I would often say that having any kind of surgery on the brain was a fear I hoped I never would have to face. And here I was preparing to be wheeled out of my hospital room to trust a surgeon to perform a craniotomy to place a VP shunt for a chance of returning to my former self. Wow, crazy isn't it?

When I woke up in my room after the surgery, my daughter Jen was there and I couldn't believe it was over. I was just so relieved that I was alive, awake, and amazed that all this took place and I was to have a second chance at life!

Jen wasn't sure that she should get a mirror to show me my shaved head. I remember her as she kept looking at the bandages and the shaved area with a little look of concern but also relief. I was fortunate to have a resident in on the surgery who was very careful about the areas she shaved. Because I had a lot of hair, she took a rather large portion of my hair and put it in a ponytail that could be used as a comb-over to cover the shaved portion. Once the incision began healing, the comb-over worked really well to cover the scars and the shaved right side of my head. It's taken two years for the regrowth of hair to catch up and I now part my hair on the opposite side.

Modeling my post-surgery shaved head. Not too bad!

The morning after my surgery, Ken was with me when Dr. Torres came in to see me. The first thing he said was, "Let's see how you are walking." I had come in using a walker. I went out into the hallway and was able to walk all the way down it without much problem dragging my right leg. As I turned around to walk back, there were my two angels, Dr. Torres and Ken, smiling big smiles and amazed at the change in my gait and balance. The outcome that I had so wanted had happened. Dr. Torres told me that things should only get better. He actually was so pleased that he wanted to send me home that day, but we bargained for one more night just to make sure that I didn't have any problems or complications from the surgery.

In my career as an x-ray technologist, I was the tech who would x-ray post-shunt surgery patients for their series films and now I was that patient. For as many pneumoencephalograms that I was a part of in the dark ages of imaging and all of the shunt series films I imaged over the years, I really never knew what these patients had gone through leading up to this type of surgery.

Sometimes I would have to do follow up shunt series films in the emergency room when patients came in with malfunctioning shunts. These were the cases when the fluid was blocked by a kink in the line or an infection or dysfunction of some kind. The patients would come in with headaches, sleeplessness, vomiting, and irritability. It's amazing that for so many years as an x-ray tech I never realized what these patients had probably dealt with for so long before their shunt placement and getting to that surgery, only to experience a malfunction that brought them back.

Yes, those stories were disturbing to think about, but in the big scheme of things, I would not have changed my mind about proceeding with a shunt placement. The quality of my life has improved so much from the daily experience of falls, confusion, walking problems, balance issues, incontinence—the whole wet, wacky, and wobbly life I was living. I have been given a new lease on life and I pray that it continues to last into my old age. I am once again able to enjoy my family and grandchildren.

I am also happy that in the whole process after becoming a depressed widow, I met a man who was willing to take a chance on me. I specifically told him I didn't want him to get involved because of my medical issues when we met. My issues were so mysterious to so many doctors, and I really wasn't sure that I was going to be able to get back to a "normal" lifestyle. Well, December 11, 2020 was the date of my rebirth!

My Christmas 2020, just 14 days after surgery, was an incredible memory for me. I had found long sleeved red Rudolph the reindeer t-shirts that said "2020 You'll Go Down in History!" and had depleted the stock, buying 15 of them. I definitely wanted a family picture with all of us in the shirts. What a fun memory after all of the medical issues I had gone through while in the middle of the Covid pandemic before finally experiencing a profound improvement in my life.

It is so fitting that I have the family picture of my support team of my family and my guy Ken at the end of the year that was 2020. That will definitely go down in history in my family's memories!

Sporting our "2020 Christmas Eve" T-shirts.

18

My Physicians Dr. Espay and Dr. Torres

I am always amazed at people who are good at putting multiple-piece puzzles together—those people who have the patience and talents to stick with the task until they succeed. Throughout my episodes and walking issues, I felt like I was a puzzle for the doctors who were trying to find the missing piece that would allow me to get the help I was so desperately searching for.

What a team I was so fortunate to find at the University of Cincinnati Medical Center and the Gardner Institute for Neuroscience. Along with this medical team, I had my personal support team that helped to push me and others to not give up looking for that missing piece. I had seen so many physicians prior to getting to Dr. Espay who were missing that important piece. My team made up of my daughter, Ken, and the rest of my family kept pushing me to keep trying. I must admit that it was not always an easy task. There were numerous times after falling and getting bruised and battered that I felt like giving up. But, I had so much to live for and, quite honestly, God was not finished with me yet.

My spiritual life took such a boost during these trials of living with NPH. I was personally touched by the hand of God through incredible believers who prayed for me and helped me get through difficult days and nights.

My home health care team in the early months of 2020 were amazing caring people who definitely saw that things weren't lining up in the puzzle of a typical knee replacement rehab. One nurse went as far as to question the neurologist I had seen prior to my knee replacement about the walking issues that had started again 5 or 6 weeks into rehab. With all of those wacky, wobbly, and wet issues. Something was wrong with my brain. It was "all in my head!" I couldn't help that it would pick and choose when the episodes would escalate. I was a puzzle that was difficult to figure out until I finally got to Dr. Espay. After a very detailed, over four-hour first visit with him and his team, he came in and said those words that were music to my ears, "I think we can help you." Thank you God for putting Dr. Espay in my path to help with yet another piece of the puzzle that we were trying to solve.

The other doctor that I learned to love and respect was Dr. Torres, my neurosurgeon. He took so many precautions to make sure that it was not going to be a mistake to put in a shunt. I really appreciated his expertise and judgment in not jumping the gun but making sure that I was indeed a viable candidate for a shunt placement. I can't thank him enough for being the physician who helped change my life with this surgery.

The city of Cincinnati is so fortunate to have the UC Gardner Neuroscience Institute. I recently had a follow up appointment with Dr. Espay who made me feel so special. He was so excited to be able to celebrate the excellent outcome of my improvement. It was encouraging to hear him say that I should probably be able to live for many years with no problems since everything had gone well for two years after the shunt placement.

Unfortunately for me, my surgeon left Cincinnati about eight months after my surgery for a position in Columbus, Ohio. He said that if I ever needed to see him I could travel up the road to Columbus and that there are many qualified surgeons at UC who could help me. Hopefully, I will never have a malfunction and need to address that situation. I have to admit that it's comforting to know I have options.

My farewell gift, made for my surgeon, Dr. Torres.

19

Meeting a Messenger

So little did I realize when I started putting pen to paper to record a memoir for my family to have, that I would end up taking on a book project.

I did take journalism in high school but never thought I was much of a writer. I was more into photojournalism, becoming a photography editor for our high school yearbook. I always enjoyed dabbling in photos, cameras, and making family memories in pictures and music videos. Perhaps that is what led me to the career choice of radiography. In the early years of radiology we were like photographers using x-ray to obtain radiographs of body parts. As a fellow technologist would always say, "Bones are our business." Of course the job was more than just x-raying bones. We had barium studies to visualize upper and lower G.I. tracts, and injected contrast medium to highlight kidneys to find stones, and contrast angiography to find blockages.

So after all that I went through to finally reach the point of the VP shunt placement and success, I was so ready to start living and traveling again after recovering from the surgery. Travel restrictions that had been in place were starting to ease up once people started getting vaccinated.

My first trip was to Indian Rocks Beach, Florida in April, 2021 with my daughter's mother-in-law. She had also lost her husband to cancer. He passed almost one year after I lost Dave. She had approached me about us traveling together to get away for a couple of weeks after I was well enough to go. So two weeks into April, we went off to the beach.

It was on this trip that I started journaling and began writing my story. At that time, I was still considering it a memoir for my family to have. After returning home, I stopped writing for a while and it wasn't until Ken and I scheduled another trip to North Carolina to visit my sister Nancy, that a very spiritual event happened on our flight.

I've often been accused of talking to strangers way too much, but I am just one of those people who feels that I never meet a stranger. Maybe because I kissed the Blarney Stone at a young age while backpacking through Ireland that I have this gift of gab. My sister tells me that when she's flying, she tries to avoid people like me. I'm trying to be better about not initiating the conversation as much for fear that others may be like my sister and I would drive them crazy!

However, on this trip I would have missed a very wonderful chance meeting. Ken had his preferred window set and I was in the middle hoping that no one would sit on the aisle. I figured I could move to the aisle seat, which I preferred, if no one took that seat. Just when I thought that might happen, a passenger came down the aisle looking for his seat—which turned out to be next to me. He was carrying what looked like a musical instrument which he put in the overhead compartment. He was also carrying a briefcase which he put under the seat in front of him.

After he got settled, I introduced myself and Ken to him. He said his name was Arnold. From what I remember, that was all the exchange of information we had until after takeoff. It was after the seatbelt sign went off that the gentleman got out his briefcase and removed a book and pen. He started to read and highlighted and underlined what seemed to be quite a lot of information. Must be good information, I remember thinking. My curiosity got the best of me, and I leaned forward to try to get a glimpse of the title of the book. It was called "How to Write a Book." That did it, I couldn't help myself. I needed to find out more about this man. I felt a nudge or urge to ask more about him.

I can't tell you how many people knew of all the things I went through prior to finally getting my diagnosis and shunt placement who had never heard of Normal Pressure Hydrocephalus. After hearing tales of my frustration of getting diagnosed and finally an answer to, not only my prayers, but also the prayers of friends and others who had known what I was going through, so many of these people would end our conversation by saying, "You should write a book!"

So could this person who was seated in the aisle seat next to me on this flight be a messenger? I mean, come on, what were the chances? I had to know more. I had to ask, so I did what I do best and tried to strike up a conversation with this man while Ken was enjoying the sights from his window seat. When the gentleman took a break from reading, I turned and told him that I couldn't help but notice the title of the book he was reading and was wondering if he was planning on writing one. It turned out that I got a wealth of information from him. He was an ordained minister, a pastor of a congregation in Cincinnati, a motivational speaker, a musician, and the founder and CEO of a company. After sharing information about himself, he asked me about my story. I shared that I was a widow traveling with my friend Ken to visit my sister in North Carolina. I told him that the title of the book he was reading caught my eye since so many people had been telling me that I should write a book to share with people who may be experiencing symptoms of Normal Pressure Hydrocephalus while never having heard of the condition.

I shared some of my medical journey with him when he asked what I would be writing about. What an interesting gentleman he turned out to be. And when I found out that he was also a minister of music in the church, our meeting became that much more interesting to me having been a music minister in the Catholic Church for quite a few years. I truly believe that there are no chance meetings.

I believe everything happens for a reason or can be a learning opportunity if we are listening. God had been working on me to get started, and I felt that it couldn't have been clearer than to have this man seated next to me to get me started. It couldn't have been more direct than the title alone, "How to Write a Book."

So, getting savvy like my adult children, I took a picture of the cover and back of the book so that I could order it when I got home. I couldn't wait for the book to arrive, and I started immediately highlighting information as soon as it arrived. The book was really helpful in helping me map out how I wanted to tell my story.

Early on when I started writing, my desire was to educate others and make people aware that NPH presents with symptoms that can mimic so many other medical and cognitive conditions. I wasn't exactly sure why some of the doctors I first saw were not convinced that a shunt would help me. But I am so happy that I had the support of my family and the will to keep trying while going through so many tests and retests to finally get the VP shunt that has allowed me to live a normal life again.

What I wasn't ready for was finding out how difficult it would be, with my adult Attention Deficit Disorder, to stay committed to getting the book finished and published. So many times I would sit down determined to finish what I had started, only to find I had a difficult time staying on task. There were so many times that I almost decided to give up because of writer's block and because I doubted my ability to share my story. Just when I would think that I'd never get it done, someone who knew my story would ask how my book was coming. That would then nudge me in the direction to get it done. As I stated previously, I originally started recording what had happened as a journal of what I went through for my family to have, particularly if it turns out that NPH is a hereditary disease. Hopefully no one else in the family will have it, but if my story could help one person out there who may read about what I went through, it will be worth the time it took to write it down for others to read.

20

Understanding My Mission

D uring my path of struggles and health issues leading to the placement of my shunt, I walked a path of uncertainties. At times on this path, I spent long nights alone on my bedroom floor after slipping off the side of the bed and finding myself unable to get up. There were also those lonely nights in strange hospital settings while I was trying to get answers to the strange symptoms I was experiencing. I found myself in desolate places, wondering if I would ever get an answer and an intervention that would help me out of this dark place I seemed to be headed.

Having been a church music minister for most of my adult life, I have many scripture-based songs rooted in my heart and soul. I feel extremely blessed to have these words to rely on when going through trials in my life. My faith has truly been strengthened by discovering daily prayer and trusting in my God. He has been my strength when I was weak and my stronghold to keep me working toward my ultimate goal of finishing this memoir so that hopefully others will learn about this condition. I also hope that it can give others consolation in their journeys with NPH.

It has been amazing to me how God has worked through me so far in getting the message out about this condition. Just recently, I received a call from a woman who is a friend of a friend who has been on this journey for two years—starting around the timeframe of my shunt placement. She was experiencing walking problems, incontinence, strange feelings in her hands, difficulty driving, and falling. She shared with me her own troubles trying to get anyone in the medical profession to react to her pleas for help.

It made me sad to hear the frustrations that she is going through. It's almost like the doctors make you feel like you're making this up and that it's "all in your head." She shared with me her worry and wondering whether she was needing a psychiatrist or psychologist. I could really sympathize with her because I was finally talking to someone I could relate to. It brought back so many of those days when I was in therapy wondering what was wrong with me. All in my head? Exactly! Those fluid-filled ventricles were doing a number on my brain. But fortunately, I got the help I needed. Now here was someone calling me to talk about her upcoming surgery. I felt it was an honor to be able to share my outcome and I was so hoping and praying that she too would be helped by the interventional surgery.

When I didn't hear from her after her surgery, I texted her to see how she was doing and to ask if it was okay to call and text her. I was so thankful when she reached out. She called and apologized that she hadn't contacted me sooner to let me know how pleased she was with her results after one week. Much like with my surgery, she was walking better and her incontinence had improved. I followed up again about three weeks after her surgery and was happy to find out that she has been feeling so much better and as her friends told her after surgery, "She has her sparkle back." I must say, I understand. It's a condition that wears you down as your brain becomes affected by the excess fluid.

We are complex individuals and are wonderfully made. It's important to remember that each of us may exhibit different symptoms with the same medical condition. Understanding that now, I know that there is a reason the doctors have to run so many tests to make sure that you are a candidate for this surgical procedure. Even though it is not a difficult neurosurgical procedure, it comes with risks. Whenever the brain is operated on, the interruption in the brain can sometimes cause more severe problems if something goes wrong. There are no guarantees that everyone will be helped from shunt placement. As it was explained to me, this is why the surgeons and the neurological team have to do such extensive testing and consultation with the patient before making the decision to operate.

In my particular case, some of the symptoms I displayed were not typical of NPH. For example, the numbness and other symptoms that I was worried might indicate that I was having TIAs or ministrokes are not generally experienced by patients with NPH. However, I found out from my conversation with my new friend that she also had numbness in her hands and had difficulty determining which hand she was feeling the sensation in. Who knows? Perhaps this may be another symptom to add to the list for NPH.

I remember trying to describe these symptoms to the neurologist and having difficulty describing how it felt. So imagine the experience of having a conversation with someone who could describe having the same numbness and the brain not recognizing which hand it was in. My numbness also involved my face and sometimes my legs in addition to my hands. Since the shunt, I have not had any of those symptoms that I thought were a TIA or a stroke. I also thought for years that I had fibromyalgia because I would wake up every day with muscle and joint pain.

Since my surgery I have felt an all-around wellness that I hadn't felt in years.

My surgeon even said to me that he doesn't fully understand why some people do better than others, but when it works, it seems to work really well. However they are still cautious about jumping in too hastily, because they have seen those cases where the patients have not been helped. In reality, they have a hard time understanding why the shunt works for some and not for all.

I must admit that I am so thankful that I was able to have the surgery and get this new lease on life. For me, it has worked! Although, I realize that there is no guarantee how long it will work, I am thankful for the two and a half years I've had so far. It was a life-changing procedure for me that gave me a fresh start at a new life.

21

My Testimony

I now look so forward every day to starting my mornings in prayer, praise, and thanksgiving. How could I not want to be thankful? For out of this journey of pain, confusion, darkness, and loss, I was able to feel rebirth with a medical victory.

It makes me so sad that my own sister Sylvia was not a candidate for the shunt placement. In my heart I feel that she may have benefitted from the fluid drain and that it may have improved her cognitive decline. This is speculation I realize, but the more I learn and have experienced myself, I can't help but think of all the people with NPH who are not diagnosed, but instead put into a nursing home. Remember, that's what one doctor told my daughter was in my future. He told us to start looking into nursing home facilities as my decline started. I'm thankful we didn't believe there was nothing that could be done. In my heart and in my head, I just knew that there was hope for a better outcome.

Every day I start the morning reading a book titled, "Jesus Calling: Enjoying Peace in His Presence." It is a leather bound book of morning meditations that a friend gave to me not long after my husband died. It has since become, for seven years, my daily read in the morning. It never gets old. The message repeats year after year and it's funny how it speaks to me differently every year in different situations. I've since subscribed to a devotional that goes along with it called "Mornings with Jesus." There are times when I am finding Jesus in the words that seem to be talking directly to me. One particular day in July of 2022 the Scripture reading for this day was Luke 21:13 (NKJV) "But it will turn out for you as an occasion for testimony." Following the scripture passage is an author's take on the scripture of the day. These words from Barbranda Lumpkins Walls struck a chord with me. She stated that she had been grateful to have a chance to share her testimony about past struggles in finding and landing a perfect job, feeling it was what she was supposed to do. She felt that you never know who she might be able to bless. Truer words have never been spoken. If I can bless one person on this journey of dealing with their own, or a family member's path with NPH, then I will feel fulfilled in why I was chosen to write this testimony of my success so far with the placement of my VP Shunt.

22

Things I Learned Along the Way

The first thing I learned on my journey with NPH was that you should always trust your gut and keep searching for an answer to what is happening to you medically. Get that second and sometimes third opinion, especially if you feel you know that what's going on is not "all in your head."

Next I have learned that it's okay to talk to strangers on an airplane. You just never know who might be the stranger with a message. One of those conversations inspired me to follow up with writing this book that may help someone find answers to medical problems that they are suffering from.

I learned that my life has now changed by meeting a man I thought I wasn't looking for. Ken is a good godly man who has been my rock and motivation to get my thoughts and memories to print. He was with me through the good, the bad, and the ugly. He stuck with me as I fell, soiled myself, couldn't walk from a baseball field to the car, got lost while driving, and shed many tears in the process. He was there for many of my doctors' appointments. He was my memory and confidant as I journeyed through this craziness that became my life. He was there to pick me up when I fell, literally, and to cheer me on through the medical maze. Somehow, I'm not sure how, he saw through that nutty person he met and decided I was worth hanging in there for.

He was there the day after my shunt surgery and witnessed the new me. Taking my first steps down that hospital hallway, within my heart and "in my head," I realized the shunt was working and he was there! I will never forget the smile on his face, and on Dr. Torres' when I turned around to walk back to my room. It was like a baby learning how to walk, but this was an adult experiencing success after years of knowing something was gradually changing my gait and my life.

That walk meant so much more than I could ever have imagined. It was like my victory lap in the race of life! There at the end were two smiling faces astonished at what they were witnessing, and I will never forget their jubilation and smiles as I "all in my head" crossed that finish line!

It's now been two and a half years since that day in December 2020. Waking up and seeing my daughter Jennifer was very special. I had made it through the operation. The fluid was continuously draining now and time would tell if it was a success. Going in there had been no guarantees that this procedure was going to be the answer to all of my problems.

Much can happen in two years. My focus is now on giving thanks every day that I wake from sleep headache free. I love starting each day in prayer. I've learned to not take anything for granted. I'm convinced my life and the outcome was the result of the power of prayer, faith in my God, and an amazing supportive family and friends I have been blessed to have in my corner during this fight. They were my rocks.

I learned that I had so much more to live for after Dave's death. I was so sad wondering if I was going to be able to move on from my grief after becoming a widow. What we had as a couple and parents and grandparents was such a special part of my life. During my time in therapy, I spent many hours talking about the special relationship we had shared. The emotions I left in the therapist's office were a good purge that was helpful in dealing with my loss. Just as I decided to move on and try to be there for my kids and grandkids, the effects of NPH were starting.

This time was difficult as it started gradually with subtle signs that something was not right. Eventually we all knew that if I was going to be around to do what I love so much, being a grandmother to these wonderful grandchildren, we needed to figure this out and hope for a miracle. Well at this point, the rest is history! I'm happy to say that I am back to being able to attend the kids' sporting events and that brings me great joy.

I love to travel and have been going on trips and cruising as much as I can since Covid precautions have lifted. I'm doing what I can while I can. Recently I've been through too many losses with close friends and family. Those Covid years were rough on family deaths and aging taking its toll.

My sister Sylvia passed in December 2021. There was a time in the early stages of writing this book that I tried reading to her what I had written. She would get agitated and didn't want to hear it. Her dementia made it difficult to communicate with her at times. What did work was music. I would visit her and we would sing old songs together. We would sit and sing and laugh and cry. It was so hard for me knowing the success I had cognitively from my shunt, and I only wished that twelve years earlier they might have helped her avoid the dementia that was probably caused by her normal pressure hydrocephalus.

The week before Sylvia passed, Nancy was able to come and be with her as she declined. The four of us sisters were able to sing Christmas carols together and Sylvia would smile as we tried to sing through our tears. We knew it wouldn't be long since she was under hospice care and many of her systems were shutting down.

She was, as we all were, preparing for the last days we would all be together. Even though we knew death was near, the news of her passing came on Christmas Eve while my family was opening gifts at my house. When I got the call, it was like time stood still and like I had the wind taken out of me by a punch in the gut. The ride to her house was with Ken and so many memories of my sister going through my thoughts and tears. She had been such a fighter most of her life starting at the age of 12. I can honestly say that I never knew anyone as brave and as beautiful as my sister Sylvia.

Her entire life was dedicated to helping others. Her beautiful smile and the way she handled adversity were admirable. She always found the good in others and, even with her severe limitations, she strived to be independent and rarely complained.

When someone is trapped in a demented brain, you never know what is going to come out of their mouth. This is how it was with my sister. She could be smiling and having a wonderful time and then go into herself and tell you to "Go to Hell!" We all knew she didn't mean it, but she couldn't help what happened with the atrophy of her brain from NPH.

I can't help but think that if I hadn't gotten the shunt placement when I did, I might have had the same fate mentally that I watched my sister and grandmother descend into. God only knows.

He wasn't done with me yet and I think he wanted me to share my story to begin a new ministry of helping others from what I learned from my own experience.

I do wonder about the potentially genetic possibility of NPH and some issues that I had in childhood and whether they might have been related to NPH. I was a bedwetter as a child and when I was in kindergarten, I would vomit almost every day before school in a bush next to the building. Trust me, I've heard stories about this my whole life from my sister Nancy.

The vomiting was also an issue when our family would go out to a restaurant. I specifically remember a local family-style restaurant, Pennington's, that was not far from our house that we occasionally went to. I remember my sisters being so embarrassed because it happened pretty often that I would vomit under the booth as we were eating. I remember hearing one sister say, "Not again. What's wrong with her?"

When I entered first grade at Saint William's parochial school, I was notorious for vomiting in the cloak room. This happened fairly often when we gathered our lunches and our coats for recess. My teacher, Sister Gabriel (a Sister of Charity), would have my sister Nancy come to my classroom to sit with me while the janitor spread green deodorized sawdust over the vomit. She sometimes had Nancy walk me home after such an incident. Nancy was not happy about having the job of leaving school and walking me home.

Sister Gabriel would then call my mother after school and tell her that she thought the problem was all in "Kathleen's little head."

Fortunately as I got older, the vomiting and urinary problems improved. Probably because Sister Gabriel scared the heck out of me by calling my mother. She had had it with me, as had my sister who would yell at me every time she got pulled from class to take me home. Looking back at these childhood memories, I wonder if these occurrences of nausea and wetting myself may have been related to hydrocephalus that wasn't severe enough to raise concern. Who knows? Back then, not as much was known about the condition.

Perhaps Sister Gabriel knew the answer to my childhood problems when she told my mother that "It's all in Kathleen's little head." She may have hit the nail on the head!

A SPECIAL RECOGNITION

There are so many people I could dedicate this book to. Hopefully you will recognize those important people as you read this memoir.

There is one person that I especially want to recognize as I finish my memoir, "It's All in Your Head, Kathleen," and that is my deceased sister Sylvia. She was truly the writer in our family of Doherty girls. It was Sylvia who had a way with words. She had a natural gift for writing and we could always count on a special poem from her for family birthdays. She also was on the staff of our Seton high school newspaper and was editor during her senior year.

As an adult, she was involved with the Polio Connection clinic committee to educate physicians about post-polio syndrome and the late effects of polio that survivors often experience as they age. She contributed a very informative article to the organization's newsletter about her experience with rehabilitation and her career as a speech pathologist in the Cincinnati community. After many years in the field, she gradually had to cut back from full-time work as she noticed her once regained physical abilities were slowly beginning to diminish due to post-polio syndrome.

Sylvia eventually went to part-time employment at University (Holmes) Hospital in the physical medicine and rehabilitation department, where she provided speech and cognitive remediation services for neurologically impaired outpatients. Her goal at

Holmes was to establish a clinic where physicians in the community would become educated about the latent effects of polio. Sylvia put it this way, "As polio survivors all of us have great track records for being able to adapt. We can continue to harness our positive thinking and adaptability to help the medical community discover solutions as we face new challenges."

The polio epidemic was particularly devastating for my sister Sylvia, but I can't help but think that out of all of us sisters, she was probably the one who was strong enough to accept her disability and adapt to her challenges. She looked at her life as being very normal and fulfilling. She felt blessed to have attended college and to enjoy a rewarding career. She felt fortunate to meet her wonderful husband, Henry, and be able to travel extensively because of him. As she put it, another "exciting dimension" was added to their lives when they adopted their daughter Rebecca at age five.

When it became too hard for Sylvia to work any longer, she found great comfort in joining a women's writing group. She was able to write about her life and share it with other women in "Read Arounds" where the writers would share their writings and critique each other. She really enjoyed her time spent with this social group of talented women. The time spent with this group was a special therapy time for her to share her thoughts with other writers.

Life was tough for my sister, but you never would have realized it because of her ability to accept the challenges that life sent her way. I am so grateful to have had her in my life and for her to have served as a role model for me when I had to deal with the curveballs life has thrown at me. She taught me patience in times of trials. I feel that she would have been proud of me for writing this memoir that I felt called to do in the hopes of helping others who may be struggling to understand NPH. I only wish that she was still with me to see the fruits of my labor and see what an inspiration she was to me.

In the way that she became an advocate for polio and post-polio survivors through her writing and advocacy work, I can only hope my story will help others to seek help for NPH.

Thank you Sylv for being my role model and for inspiring me to even attempt writing this memoir, for not only my family, but also for others to get an understanding of this condition that is often able to be successfully treated. My hope is that my story may help others to regain a normal life, as I did, with the placement of a ventricular peritoneal shunt.

Love,
Your baby sister Kathleen (aka Kathy Sue)

PERSONAL UPDATE

As I make the final edits on my memoir, I will be coming up on three years post shunt placement.

I am pleased to report that my life has truly been blessed with health and happiness again!

I still have sadness over the loss of my husband and soulmate Dave, who was taken from me and our adult children too soon in our estimation. There are not many days that go by that I don't wish he was still here to enjoy our family and our wonderful grandchildren. I can't help but think he is able to watch over us and smile at what we, with the help of God, were able to create.

Our kids are raising wonderful families of their own. I love them all and I am so happy to once again get to share in their accomplishments. It was the strength and support they all provided me during those difficult times I was experiencing that gave me the will to pick myself up and try to find answers.

I hope this book will accomplish what I intended-to inform others about NPH and the improvement I experienced through treatment.

For all these blessings I am eternally grateful, and hope and pray I continue to experience long term success, and be a witness to the results I have been gifted to receive.